CALL CENTER AGENT MOTIVATION AND COMPENSATION

The Best of
Call Center Management Review

Call Center Press

A Division of ICMI, Inc.

Published by:
Call Center Press
A Division of ICMI, Inc.
P.O. Box 6177
Annapolis, Maryland 21401 USA

Printed in the United States of America

ISBN 0-9709507-3-X

Table of Contents

Foreword

The call center has evolved into a highly visible, multichannel, customer-focused environment. To be successful in this prominent role in the organization, call centers must focus on retaining and developing capable, skilled agents.

What is it that motivates agents to perform at their top level? And, importantly, what makes top performers want to stay? Paying a competitive wage that reflects the value of the individual's skills, effort and impact on the organization is a good foundation. But it doesn't end there. The call centers that are able to retain experienced staff have also implemented programs for skills-based compensation, incentives and career development.

The articles in this collection focus squarely on these vital topics. Originally published in the pages of *Call Center Management Review*, they were selected for their educational value, practicality and, most importantly, coverage of timeless call center management principles.

We hope you enjoy the book!

Sincerely,
The ICMI Team

Chapter 1:
Motivation

Fancy Titles, More Responsibility Won't Keep Agents

Government Call Centers Share Tips for Improving Morale and Motivation

Improving Call Center Performance Through People

Bank of America Honors Top Reps at One-of-a-Kind Company Conference

Dealing with the "Free-Agent" Mindset: Rethink Recruiting and Rewards

Fancy Titles, More Responsibility Won't Keep Agents

by Fay Wilkinson

Today, we have a real opportunity to do things differently. We're used to it; our call centers are breaking new ground every day.

I suspect one of the reasons call center managers consider career paths is to bring legitimacy to our profession. After all, if there's a defined hierarchical structure, then surely we'll be accepted within our organizations? Right? Perhaps.

I suggest we dare to ask: Why do we need traditional career paths? To acknowledge/reward agents for progress? To stop them from leaving? To give them more money/status? To provide variety and prevent boredom? There are other ways to accomplish those objectives. It's time to turn our organizational compass from vertical to horizontal.

What call centers actually need are skilled, energized people who will embrace a variety of new functions with associated skills and knowledge sets. What we want to encourage and value is the development and consistent demonstration of these skills at a superior level. A one-day course does not an expert make. And, yes, as people become more valuable to us we need to pay them accordingly.

So now we're hearing about skill-pathing rather than career-pathing. This fits well with the new generation of "Nexters" coming soon to a call center near you. They are considered to be the most educated generation so far; they are technologically savvy; and their job will be only one factor in their lives, so a fancy title and loads of responsibility may not be high on their priority list.

And no, they won't be staying with you forever no matter what you do. There are some call centers that are being creative, innovative and, frankly, realistic. There simply aren't enough team leader/management jobs for everyone. My hat is off to them. They're on the right track.

Government Call Centers Share Tips for Improving Morale and Motivation

by Leslie Hansen Harps

Improving morale in your call center and providing an environment that meets your agents' needs can pay off in increased employee retention and improved customer satisfaction.

"Truly successful call centers appreciate that call center representatives are the ultimate link to a healthy, productive center," says Terry J. Clements, director of the Social Security Administration's (SSA) Albuquerque Teleservice Center. In the call center, "we have the very strong urge to focus on systems, productivity and management information," he continues. "Yet the real focus should be — and must be — on supporting the people who work with customers in a very stressful environment."

Offering call center employees a competitive benefits and compensation package, while important, simply builds the foundation for happy, satisfied staffers. Other key elements to take into consideration include:

• **Hiring.** All the motivational programs in the world won't help you retain an agent who is poorly suited to work in a call center. Structure your interview process so that it enables you to screen out these candidates. "Using carefully engineered questions that call for specific examples can help you develop insight as to whether or not the candidate has qualities, such as genuine concern for customers, acting as part of a team, and the ability to learn quickly," Clements says.

The SSA Teleservice Center found that involving management and union reps in the interviewing process "improves the ability to recruit new employees who hold values that are more easily adaptable to the work culture," he observes. Some of the things they look for: the ability to handle stress, a sense of humor and flexibility.

It's also a good idea to include in the interviewing process an opportunity for candidates to get a true picture of the environment and what it's really like to work there . This will enable them to make an educated decision about whether or not it's a good match for them.

Chapter 1

- **Orientation.** Once you hire an agent, start the relationship off on a positive note with an effective orientation to your organization and to the job. By giving new-hires the information they need to get acclimated, helping them to feel comfortable in the new environment and demonstrating your interest in and appreciation of them, you help to validate their decision to join your organization during the critical first days of the relationship.

"The time to acquaint new employees with the call center's vision, values, mission and culture is immediately," Clements says. He and the call center's assistant manager invest several hours leading an interactive discussion with new-hires on values and expectations of employees, their supervisors and customers. "It helps to get things started on the right foot."

During their new-hire orientation, the New York State (NYS) Department of Tax and Finance, Tax Compliance Division call centers set a positive tone — and demonstrate the call center's importance to the organization. Division Director Joe Gecewicz and other key managers personally welcome the new staff during the orientation and let them know what to expect. So that new tax compliance representatives can be more easily be assimilated into the call center, they're hired in small groups of 20.

Another suggestion: Consider assigning mentors or buddies during an employee's first days with your organization to provide guidance and information, and to make your new-hires feel welcome. This can be a motivator for both the experienced agent as well as the new-hire.

- **The work environment.** Also consider the environment in which your agents work, advises John DeFiore. A tax compliance manager with the New York State Department of Tax and Finance, Tax Compliance Division, he oversees two call centers that employ some 300 people. "Problems such as isolation and loneliness, as well as work pace and turnover are common in many centers," he says.

Factors such as these were affecting morale in the NYS call centers, where agents were "bound by a headset, and with minimal opportunity for social interaction." To improve the workplace and enhance morale, the centers took a number of steps, including:

1. Enhancing the work space with new paint and furniture;

2. Combining team meetings when possible to give individual team members an opportunity to meet others within the center; and

3. Actively participating in a very successful department-wide event called TAXPO, an in-house exposition that featured displays from the various units in the department. The event gave call center agents the opportunity to learn about the functions of other units — and vice versa — and helped them to understand where they fit in the overall organization.

• **Training.** Providing continual learning is motivational for teleservice reps and beneficial for the call center. "The better we can create an environment where people are challenged, and provide opportunities where people learn and grow, the more successful we'll be," according to Clements. Both the NYS Tax Compliance call centers and SSA Teleservice Center have dedicated trainers who conduct sessions for experienced call center representatives as well as new-hires.

Recognizing that it can be difficult to fit time for training into a busy call center, the SSA Teleservice Center has established the position of "gatekeeper," an individual who coordinates time for training. "It's not always easy to find the time to train," Clements says, "but you have to develop teleservice reps so that they can grow."

Employees at the teleservice center receive ongoing skills and program training. They also listen to guest speakers or receive training on topics such as celebrating diversity.

• **Career advancement/job enrichment.** As government organizations, the NYS Tax Compliance and SSA call centers both have very clear, well-defined career paths. For example, at the SSA Teleservice Center — which has some 600 employees — reps can compete to become a technical assistant, then compete to become a supervisor. In addition to advancing through this career path to management, reps also can compete to move into the center's 50-person claims unit, which gives them broader opportunities for advancement.

In addition, employees at the center can find variety in a number of different ways, Clements points out. "We provide opportunities for teleservice employees to do different kinds of work, such as working in a field office or a contact station where customers are assisted in person rather than by phone." Call center employees are selected to serve on task forces, and to participate in different pilot programs. Reps can also undergo training to become instructors.

• **Rewards and recognition.** The NYS Tax Compliance call centers, like others in the state tax/finance department, are encouraged to recognize the contributions of their peers through Star Awards and Thank-You notes programs. Managers and supervisors can handwrite their commendations using a Star Award, a document about the size of an index card printed with a gold star. The award is given to the individual who performs an extraordinary action, DeFiore explains. Pre-printed Thank-You notes also make it easy for staff members to handwrite their thanks to staff member in any department who has assisted them in some way.

The SSA Teleservice Center has several recognition programs, including a Giraffe Award to recognize individuals who "stick their necks out" to serve a customer. "They can be nominated by peers or their supervisor," Clements explains. Those who receive the award are presented with a small toy giraffe during a special ceremony.

At the Teleservice Center, cash awards can be given to recognize exceptional individual accomplishments. But Clements believes that "providing challenges, a learning environment where the individual feels that he or she has control, and a supporting atmosphere where employees have a sense of involvement, plus friends at work, are much more important than cash rewards."

• **Fun.** The NYS call centers strive to make work fun for their employees. Activities include an Ice Cream Social, as well as contests and special events, such as a Sports Day Dress-Up contest, a Hat Day, Guess the Call Center Stats contest, and Halloween costume and holiday decorating contests. "The contests have proven extremely popular and participation increases with every contest," according to DeFiore. But "while we have made great efforts to make work fun, we have not lost sight of our mission," he says.

Terry Clements agrees. "You can do serious work without taking yourself too seriously." The SSA Teleservice Center has a range of activities that include cookouts, potlucks, functions featuring different types of ethnic foods, Tae Bo classes, even lessons taught by the union president, an experienced folklorico dancer.

• **Management.** Recognizing the significant impact management can have on morale and motivation, managers at the NYS tax compliance call centers agreed to maintain an open-door policy. Managers at one center moved to cubicles placed in the middle of the floor, which improved access and eliminated perceived barriers between managers and the front line.

Managers at the NYS centers also encourage open communication. For example, frontline supervisors solicit ideas from and concerns of their team members during coaching sessions. These are later discussed with managers, with each idea considered and a response given.

Call center staffers can also use suggestion boxes throughout the center. Suggestions are discussed at manager meetings, and a response developed. The suggestions and responses are posted on the organization's Intranet, which was built by frontline staff. The Intranet also contains procedure manuals and resources, plus items of general interest to the call center team.

Managers make a concerted effort to involve staff at all levels, such as when working on the TAXPO, developing the organization's Intranet, or working on procedures. "Managers have empowered our staff to lead in the call center's continuing development," reports John DeFiore. "The staff has responded with many enhancements to the collective work environment." As call center employees' feelings of accomplishment increase, so do the levels of job satisfaction, which leads to increased morale.

Benefits include better attendance and higher occupancy rates. "We're able to handle more calls and provide customer service," DeFiore says. "The many complimentary letters we've received provide the proof that our efforts at improving morale have been worthwhile."

Improving Call Center Performance Through People

by Christian M. Ellis and Elizabeth J. Hawk

Call centers drive higher sales and better margins when they are viewed by management as a significant lever of organizational performance.

To gain recognition from upper management, as well as the commitment and loyalty needed from agents, managers have to concentrate on several key areas, such as defining the call center's overall function and mission; developing fair and attainable performance metrics and goals for agents; and developing a compelling employee value proposition.

Define the Role of the Call Center

If you want your call center to be competitive, your agents need to fully understand the mission they're being asked to undertake. For call center leadership, this means clearly stating why their unit exists, what it contributes to the larger business and what appropriate measures will be used to assess its success. In addition, leaders need to develop and communicate a detailed plan for future contribution to the company's overall performance. Without such clarity of vision, the call center cannot hope to successfully compete for the resources and recognition that it will need over time.

Some call centers have been successful in broadening the view of the value they deliver to the larger organization. They can describe their value as: 1) customer relationship management, 2) revenue support, and 3) marketplace sensing to support new product development.

Developing a wider range of success measures allows call centers to reap dual benefits: 1) top management views them as a more critical part of the business, with all the favorable implications for attention and resources; and 2) they are able to motivate their staff with much more engaging missions and goals.

Develop Fair and Attainable Performance Metrics/Goals

Six Tips for Creating Financial Rewards

There are several rules of thumb in developing financial rewards that drive agent retention and performance:

- Attract necessary talent with a competitive starting rate of pay.
- Provide substantial pay growth opportunity through a skills/knowledge-based pay progression system.
- Provide flexibility for agents to develop capabilities at their own pace and to focus on areas of expertise that interest them.
- Retain more experienced agents with a competitive living wage.
- Motivate and inspire through focused incentive programs that reward unit/team results.
- Provide significant bonus opportunity for achieving stretch results.

A service-oriented center moving beyond the traditional cost-focused "reason for being" will find itself in need of new ways to track performance. In a customer service call center, this might mean moving beyond measures like cost per call, calls handled per hour or average handle time. The productivity focus of these measures is not bad, but it's just not balanced. The drive tends to be viewed as "get 'em off the phone as quickly as possible" and move on to the next call.

Reps respond well to having the quality (not just quantity) of their work measured. Attention to internal quality measures is one approach, which includes:

- Process compliance checks — were all of the steps prescribed for the task, in fact, completed?
- Output checks — did the agent complete the task accurately and was response timely?

Many centers are also adding external quality assessment to their routine measures of performance. This typically involves three steps:

1. Find out what's important to your customers. Is it the speed with which a customer service call is answered? Or do customers care most about getting their problems diagnosed accurately and solved completely? Or is the key whether or not the agent demonstrates empathy and concern for the caller? Note that expectations will vary based on the kind of service being provided to customers, as well as by type of caller.

2. Determine the level of performance customers expect. Is an answer within three rings expected, or is five sufficient? What are the ways an agent can demonstrate the expected level of concern for the customer? Again, these will vary by type of work and by customer type.

3. Find out how agents are currently performing against these standards and how to improve. The call center measures performance, then peels apart its processes and enhances them to meet customer expectations.

Creating a Compelling Employee Value Proposition

Most call center managers would agree that agent satisfaction and retention is directly correlated with customer satisfaction and retention. Yet many frontline employees believe that their company is not doing a good job of meeting their needs.

In a study by Sibson & Co., called *Rewards of Work*, more than 70 percent of frontline workers indicated they were committed to the success of their organization. However, only 51 percent believed their organizations truly cared about their general satisfaction.

However, satisfying agents — motivating, supporting and rewarding them in meaningful ways — has become increasingly difficult for several reasons. First, the workforce is becoming more diverse demographically, bringing with it a great diversity of employee needs, values and cultural norms. Second, the workforce is becoming more diverse structurally with full-time, part-time and temporary employees, as well as subcontractors often working side-by-side in one call center. Finally, job opportunities in tight labor markets create a war for talent that makes it easy for agents to "jump ship" for better opportunities.

To improve agent commitment, satisfaction and, ultimately, retention and performance, develop a flexible and differentiating employee value proposition. A comprehensive value proposition clearly spells out the beliefs, policies and practices of the organization in creating a meaningful and inspiring work environment. It also answer the questions "Why do agents want to work in the center?" and "Why should they want to stay?" It involves both financial and nonfinancial rewards (see the Rewards of Work Model illustrated below).

The Rewards of Work Model

People do work for more than just money. The Rewards of Work model shows the five elements of any reward system — two are financial; three are not.

Call centers should address all five elements and find out from their agents what they truly value. Achieving this balanced approach will enable you to differentiate your call center from others, motivate high-performing agents to increase their effectiveness and help to resist the temptation of the (not so green) grass on the other side of the fence.

Affiliation
• Organizational reputation
• Company culture
• Work environment
• Corporate citizenship

Direct Financial
• Base salary
• Incentives
• Ownership
• Cash recognition
• Premiums

Rewards of Work

Work Content
• Variety/challenge
• Accountability
• Work schedule
• Meaningfulness
• Performance feedback

Indirect Financial
• Benefits
• Noncash recognition
• Perquisites

Career
• Organizational advancement
• Training and development
• Employment security
• Personal growth

Achieving the Right Balance of Rewards

Often, call center pay systems reward people for showing up, staying and working fast, rather than for providing high-quality service and high levels of customer satisfaction.

While there is much talk about variable or incentive pay programs, these approaches will only be successful if other basic rewards are present, including a "living wage"—a paycheck substantial enough to cover the cost of living—and solid healthcare benefits. Keeping close track of wage and compensation trends is critical, especially in low unemployment labor markets where the competition for talent is high.

But a meaningful employee value proposition is about more than just money. It is also about sincerely convincing agents that they belong to a great organization and that their work is truly valued.

This affiliation is easier to sell in some organizations than in others. Some centers may be able to tap into the strong cultural presence of the broader organization. However, others will need to develop employee affiliation within the center itself.

Probably the most compelling approach is to develop a customer-focused culture. Call center agents can more easily get excited about working in an environment that emphasizes customer delight than one focused on maximizing profits for the company. Why? Because they can see the impact on their customers daily but often don't see the bottom-line impact for the company.

Perhaps the most critical step in creating a differentiating and sustaining value proposition is to design work that is meaningful, challenging, has variety and requires teaming or interaction with others.

Improving the work content of jobs is also a great first step in providing a meaningful career element to the value proposition. Studies have shown that agents care about learning new skills, taking on greater responsibilities and strengthening their overall employability.

Perhaps more importantly, they want a reasonably stable environment where they know they will have a job if they perform to expectations. Managers who overlook agent career needs and goals risk high turnover and poor performance.

Bank of America Honors Top Reps at One-of-a-Kind Company Conference

by Greg Levin

Chapter 1

In mid-June, Bank of America's (BA) five California call centers lost more than 200 of their best reps for two days. No, their absences weren't caused by a flu that only affects top-performers, but by a unique company conference that honors them.

It's called the "Bankers On Call Conference," which BA developed to recognize agents who provide outstanding customer service and exceed company sales objectives. The conference is held each year at a different hotel in Southern California. During their two days off the phones, the elite agents compete in group games, listen to motivational speeches from senior management, attend an award ceremony honoring the "best of the best," and let loose at an exciting dinner bash. In addition to the agents, at least one manager from each call center attends the annual conference.

While the focus of the conference is on fun, important information is delivered to the agents.

"It's not only a great way to show our top agents how much we appreciate their outstanding performance," explains Diane Pasiuk, conference organizer and manager of BA's Glendale center, "we can deliver messages that are pertinent to their jobs and to their success in the call center. They can then pass this information on to their colleagues when they return to their call centers."

The six California inbound call centers from which attendees are chosen are located in Glendale (which also houses an inbound/outbound sales unit), Orange County, San Bernardino, Pleasant Hill and Fresno. Of the 1,800 agents who work in these centers, 230 were invited to attend this year's festivities, which were held at the Red Lion Hotel in Glendale, Calif., and Paramount Movie Studios in Hollywood. Last year's conference was held at the Hilton Hotel in Burbank and Universal Studios in Universal City.

Selecting Stars, Filling Staffing Gaps

All agent attendees are selected by the managers at their respective centers. Managers determine who the top-performers are based on monitoring results, employee evaluations and general observations of the agents at work. "We look for real service leaders, the agents who go beyond the norm," says Pasiuk. "We consider customer service first, then sales." She adds that top-sellers who don't meet the general service criteria will not be selected to go to the conference.

BA does not have "set-in-stone" criteria or sales numbers that agents must meet to receive a conference invitation. "We trust that managers know who the 'stars' are just from observing them every day," says Pasiuk. "We leave the selection process up to each call center. We don't want to reduce the selection process to, 'You had to have a score of X to qualify.'"

Despite the relatively informal selection criteria, agents seem satisfied with the process. "I have not heard of any complaints about unfair office politics with regard to who gets to go to the conference," says Pasiuk. "It's usually obvious to everybody who deserves an invitation. If we could possibly invite more agents, we would, but we still have a business to run."

And running the call centers without the company's top performers can be a challenge. During BA's first conference two years ago, each call center maintained its normal staffing level by scheduling just enough agents to cover the conference attendees. However, the centers still struggled to maintain their normal service levels. "We had a full schedule, but didn't consider the effect of not having the 'best of our best,'" Pasiuk recalls. "As a result, our handle time went up and we weren't able to take as many calls as usual."

BA solved the problem this year by overstaffing to compensate for the missing top performers. "That worked much better," says Pasiuk.

This Year's Event a Blast for Agents

Those agents selected this year got to travel through time, as the theme of the conference was "Blast to the Future." As the agents piled into the large hotel auditorium for the first conference session, they gazed at a futuristic stage and stars on the walls while listening to Neil Diamond's "We're Headed for the Future" pumping in through speakers.

Don Owen, senior vice president and head of California Statewide Teleservices for BA, kicked off the conference with a talk and a slide show on where BA's call centers have been, how far they've come and where they are headed. While the emphasis was on how the call center technology has evolved and improved, Owen ended his presentation with the importance of customer service and of building rapport with each customer.

The next speaker, Robert Menicucci—executive vice president and region manager for BA—continued the customer service message. Menicucci, who manages many of BA's retail branches, talked about the similarities involved in handling a customer in person at a branch or over the phone at a call center. He reminded the agents that it's important for the company to work together to provide unparalleled customer service regardless of the channel customers choose.

Following a picnic lunch outside the hotel, the agents were split into three groups that rotated through three breakout sessions. Two of the sessions covered BA products and tested agents' knowledge using game show themes. "One of the sessions had a Family Feud theme and the other had a Jeopardy theme," says Pasiuk. "These were rousing, very loud and energetic product knowledge sessions! Agents were leaping around and yelling, bells were ringing. They had a blast and learned while they played." Winners received prizes, including shirts and other giveaways as well as money.

The third breakout session focused on service and included scripted role-plays of common customer situations. To add a little competition into the mix, agents in each group were divided into teams, with managers rating their performance. Agents were rated on their ability to recognize and take advantage of upselling and cross-selling opportunities, as well as their ability to build rapport with customers. "This session, while not as wild and upbeat as the others, was probably the most important of the three [breakout sessions]," says Pasiuk.

After the three agent groups completed all three breakout sessions, they reunited in a general session. The speaker was Barbara Desoer, group executive vice president for BA's California retail banking division. "Barbara is the most senior person in our California retail structure," Pasiuk points out. "Like the previous speakers at the conference, she talked about the importance of exceeding customer expectations and building relationships with customers. The message was similar to Don and Robert's, but came from a much more senior level. This showed agents that our entire organization is serious about a strong focus on customer service."

Desoer's presentation was followed by a "Q&A" session. Pasiuk admits that she and the other managers had "planted" some questions with agents to ensure that the session didn't bomb, but the managers later found that they had underestimated the agents' curiosity. "The group had so many of their own questions! They didn't need any of ours," Pasiuk says.

Space Suits and Poodle Skirts

In addition to speeches and games, some of the call center managers acted in little stage skits throughout the afternoon to reinforce the importance of customer service. For example, one skit that took place on two stages compared BA's call center past to its future. On one stage, a manager portrayed a character named "Pokey from the Past." "Pokey fumbled around trying to locate a branch, doing all kinds of silly things," explains Pasiuk. "He searched a blown-up map of the world with a magnifying glass in an attempt to find it, and interacted very comically with the customer on the phone." The skit then switched over to the second stage, which featured an agent wearing a spacesuit working at a "Jetson-like" workstation. This agent used "Branch Locator" technology to smoothly handle the caller's request. "There were all sorts of funny exaggerations of how advanced our service will be in the future," says Pasiuk. "For example, the technology the agent used not only told him where the branch was, it provided local traffic information so the agent could tell the caller the quickest way to get there."

At the evening event—a dinner/dance party at Paramount Movie Studios—spacesuits were traded in for leather jackets and poodle skirts. While the overall conference theme was "Blast to the Future," the party theme was "Blast to the Past." "We made it clear to all the agents that the event was going to be strictly social and fun, no business," says Pasiuk. The managers held true to their promise. The '50s theme party included a bubble-gum blowing contest, a hula-hoop contest and a Jitterbug dance contest. Pasiuk was impressed with agents' costumes. "Pretty darn close to 100 percent of the agents got into the '50s spirit," she says.

Honoring the Best of the Best

The next morning, agents traveled back to the present for the final hours of the conference, featuring an agent award ceremony that honored the stars among the stars. Three agents from each of BA's six California call centers (18 agents in total) received recognition for "exceptional performance" during the prior year. Among these winners was an agent who consistently achieves the highest monitoring scores, receives numerous customer comments and helps agents who struggle with service issues. The top salesperson in the state was also among the honored agents. All winners were called up to the stage individually, with their names appearing on a big screen in the front of the auditorium while the song "Best of the Best" filled the room. These agents were each given a clock with a marble base on which their names were engraved.

Don Owen closed the year's conference by reminding agents how important it was for them to take their enthusiasm and knowledge back to the call center. "He told them that we needed them to be ambassadors back at their respective call centers," says Pasiuk.

The agents have done just that. "They [the agents who didn't attend the conference] were very curious about all that happened at the conference when I returned," says Cynthia Salazar, a customer service rep at BA's Glendale call center who attended the Bankers On Call event. "I was able to share what knowledge I brought back."

To enhance the information that attendees passed on to their fellow agents back at their centers, BA videotaped the entire conference for all to see. Pasiuk and other managers edited the video to include the highlights—the key messages presented as well as some of the more humorous and entertaining parts. Team leaders will soon be showing the recently completed video to agents during team meetings and discussing the information covered at the conference. "We put a lot of effort—and money—into the conference, so we want to make sure that it benefits as many employees as possible," Pasiuk explains. "Enabling the agents [who weren't selected] to see what happened increases the value of the conference and motivates agents to work harder so that they have a chance to be invited the following year."

Agents Wowed by Royal Treatment

Pasiuk realizes that she is lucky to work for a company with the funds and call center commitment required to put on such an elaborate conference for agents each year. The agents feel even luckier.

"They are absolutely 'wowed' to be invited to a nice hotel for an overnight event, to be treated royally with great food and entertainment and to get a chance to interact with senior management," says Pasiuk. "They see how much we appreciate the great work they do for us."

Agent Salazar was so impressed she's determined to attend the 1998 conference. "It was spectacular, she says. "The content was outstanding and I was extremely honored to be able to attend. I am going to do all I can to be invited next year."

Dealing with the "Free-Agent" Mindset: Rethink Recruiting and Rewards

by Susan Hash

The Generation X mindset became a strong force in the workplace in the early 1990s, challenging corporate cultures and rejecting the traditional button-down management policies and procedures.

Just when companies were learning how to adjust to their Generation X workforce (now 24 to 39 years of age), along comes the next wave of call center agents— Generation Y.

Generation Y includes 68 million Americans born between 1977 and 1994 (workers 16 to 24 years of age), 40 million of whom are already in the workforce.

"All of those disconcerting attitudes and behaviors that Corporate America had to learn to work with for Generation X have been challenged. It's created even more of a necessary mind-meld for managers to work with the emerging generation," says Eric Chester, author of *And You Thought Generation X Was Tough*, and founder of Generation Why. Chester coined the phrase "Generation Why" to better describe this generation, which "is typified by youth who continually question the standards and expectations imposed by society," (i.e., "why does it matter?" and "why should I care?").

Like the preceding generation, Generation Y is changing the way business has to function and operate, says Chester.

Generation Y can be described as "similar to Generation X—only on fast forward," says Bruce Tulgan, author of *Managing Generation Y* and founder of Rainmaker Thinking Inc., a research firm focused on the working lives of Americans born after 1963. "They're the self-esteem generation. Their independence isn't fierce, it's casual. They know they'll have to take care of themselves and they're not worried at all."

The Staffing Crisis Is Not Going to End

While the Generation Y workforce will surely impact businesses in upcoming years, Tulgan points out that some 20 million older Gen Xers are now managers. "They're already doing things differently," he says.

He adds that the key changes in business were brought about by business leaders and management experts who began to change the employer-employee relationship more than a decade ago through reengineering, downsizing and restructuring. "It's not just young workers who know they have to fend for themselves in this environment. Employers no longer offer job security, so employees of all ages are starting to think like free agents." The free-agent mindset is possibly the biggest challenge that employers have ever had to deal with, Tulgan says.

"That means managing people is going to be much harder than it's ever been. You

Understanding the Generational Perspectives			
	Baby Boomers 1946-1960	**Generation X** 1961-1976	**Generation Why** 1977-1994
The Future	"Is ours!"	"Sucks!"	"Ain't gonna happen."
Wealth	"I'll earn it."	"I don't want it."	"Gimme, or I'll take it."
Employment	"Lucky to find."	"Only if I have to."	"Jobs are a dime a dozen."
Loyalty	"To the end!"	"For a while."	"Until a better offer."
Instruction	"Tell me WHAT to do."	"Show me HOW to do it."	"WHY do I need to know!"
Communication	Via parent's phone	Via personal phone	Pager/cell phone/ email
Change	Dislike	Accept	Demand
Technology	Ignorant	Comfortable	Masters of
Video Game	Pong	PacMan	Mortal Kombat

Source: Eric Chester, Generation Why, Web site: www.generationwhy.com

won't be able to retain people; we're going to have a staffing crisis on our hands forever. Instead, you need to change the way you do business," he says.

Bill Peters, VP of reservations for Outrigger Hotels in Denver, agrees. "There's really no commitment [among younger staff] to the business for the long term," he says. However, he attributes part of that to the job market. "If the economy was down, people would spend more time trying to achieve more in their current positions instead of just jumping ship with the first confrontation or poor performance review."

Rethinking Recruiting Strategies

Recruiting is the key process call center managers should consider revamping right away. "In the workplace of the future, you're not looking for people to join the family or climb the ladder," says Tulgan. "Rather, you need people who bring specific skills to the table, who are able to get up to speed quickly and who can begin making valuable contributions right away."

Outrigger Hotels is changing its recruiting process to focus on agents who fit a particular profile—specifically, candidates attending local technical or travel schools, or those interested in getting into the hospitality industry. "We focus on those people trying to get their degrees—sending the message that this would be a great job for them for a year or so," says Sandy Schuster, Outrigger's director of human resources.

"It's not fair to say this would be a great career for you," adds Peters. "But if we can identify that profile during or prior to the interview process, we have a better chance of retaining that employee for at least a year." The call center's goal is to retain 65 to 70 percent of its agents for a year.

Reaching the Right Candidates

Because of the tight labor market, many call centers are so desperate to hire agents that the main selection criterion appears to be whether or not they have a pulse, says Tulgan. Besides changing the recruiting focus to a more short-term outlook, "the goal of developing a compelling recruiting message and running an effective cam-

> **Additional Resources**
>
> Articles and information on the Gen X and Y workforce are available online:
>
> - Find out more about Generation "Why" at www.generationwhy.com.
> - Read about the "free agent" mindset at www.rainmakerthinking.com.

paign is to attract an applicant pool that's large enough to allow you to be selective," he says.

At FurstPerson, a call center outsourcing firm in Chicago, recruiting has become a sales and marketing strategy, says Vice President Michelle Cline.

"We've had to take a hard look at the marketing tactics we use to go after candidates in the younger age groups. It has forced us to reallocate some of our resources away from traditional recruiting mechanisms to investing in more Internet and grassroots type of recruiting."

FurstPerson's agent recruiting campaign targets places that Gen Xers and Yers frequent, such as coffee houses, movie theaters and outdoor activities like beach volleyball.

"It does take a little more effort to shake out the right candidates," says Outrigger's Schuster. Her company has expanded its recruiting sources from just using newspaper ads to including radio advertising, job fairs, local community colleges and Internet ads.

An effective recruiting campaign must be both aggressive and year-round, adds Tulgan. "That means all company materials, even sales materials should be developed with your recruiting goals in mind." He offers the following four basic elements and suggestions for developing an effective campaign:

- **Unpaid media (news or quasi-news coverage).** Develop concrete news stories or events to pitch to editors and reporters by building a list of all the potential angles and events that are newsworthy about your recruiting program. Don't dismiss unconventional tactics such as letters to the editor and calls to phone-in talk shows.

- **Paid media (advertising).** The key to an effective ad in any media is being disciplined about sticking to the message. Don't just consider print ads. Write a script for a 60-second radio spot, buy a 30-second spot on cable television or place your ad online at a job posting Web site.

Build a Fluid Talent Pool to Leverage Staffing ROI

The demand for talent will continue to outpace the supply for the foreseeable future, says Bruce Tulgan. And "there's no doubt that most employers are experiencing the staffing crisis most acutely with their youngest workers."

To combat high turnover, Tulgan suggests call center managers work on developing a "fluid talent pool."

"When agents leave, don't let them leave altogether. Put them in your reserve army," he says. "Offer them the chance to continue adding value on a part-time basis, as flex-timers, telecommuters, periodic temps or consultants. Let them leave and come back in three months, six months or a year." Keep a list of names and phone numbers of high-performing agents. When you have a staffing gap, call your former employees and ask if they would like to come in and work—full time or on a temporary basis.

Then, welcome them back with open arms. "After all," he says. "You've already invested in recruiting and training them, why not leverage your investment?"

- **Direct contact (mail, telephone, fax, email).** Identify and secure available databases with accurate contact information. Decide which means of direct contact will be most effective for reaching those people.

- **Events (sponsored by you or someone else).** When planning events, keep in mind: 1) What can you do to make the event special to your target market, and 2) What is the potential news/publicity tie-in?

Immediate Gratification Is Key

When it comes to compensation, both Generations X and Y expect to be paid what they think they're worth. The main difference between the younger generations and their Baby Boomer predecessors is the period or intervals at which incentives or rewards are expected.

"These groups don't tolerate annual bonuses or reviews," says FurstPerson's Cline. "They want instant gratification from a financial standpoint, as well as with feedback on performance."

Cline says that bonuses at her company have dropped from yearly to quarterly or even monthly. In addition to monetary compensation, Gen X and Y agents value frequent pay-outs on motivational programs, such as monthly, weekly or even daily.

A roundtable discussion of Outrigger Hotel's agents revealed that, while they like having incentives to shoot for, they prefer those that have monetary value, says Assistant Director of Operations Eric Boyd. "We've offered movie tickets, gift certificates of varying amounts, plus drawings for trips."

What Works Besides Money?

While incentives are great, it takes more than that to motivate the younger workforce, says Chester.

"This is a generation who wants to have contact with a superior to let them know, on an ongoing basis, what they're doing is good."

Also, he says, given the choice between money and flexibility, they would take the freedom—wider parameters, more responsibility, less structure.

Surveys by Rainmaker Thinking found the six top choices of non-monetary rewards among 20-somethings to be:

1. Control over their work schedules.
2. Training opportunities.
3. Exposure to decision makers.
4. Credit for projects.
5. Increased responsibility.
6. Opportunities for creative expression.

"In a call center environment, where it's hard to give agents control over their own schedules, the style of the manager also makes a huge difference," says Tulgan. "Managers need to be right in there, rolling up their sleeves and engaging people."

That's true, says Schuster. Younger agents "are looking more at their managers, making sure they walk the talk—in other words, don't ask me to do something you wouldn't do."

And Bill Peters suggests managers readily accept the questioning they're likely to get from their staff. "There's a lot of thought that goes into that questioning," he says. "It used to be that agents were accountable to their managers. But in today's business environment, managers have to be accountable to their staff."

Chapter 2:
Compensation

Call Center Professionals Speak Up for Underpaid Agents

Agent Compensation: Motivating Staff without Burying Budgets

Skills-Based Pay Program Raises Performance and Lowers Costs

A Candid Conversation on Call Center Compensation

Call Center Professionals Speak Up for Underpaid Agents

by Greg Levin

Lately, everywhere you look there is a business magazine or report telling how companies consider their call centers to be of vital importance—the key to customer retention, increased profits and market share. Companies are investing more in technology and training, and requiring that agents do more to keep up with increasing customer demands. Gone are the days when companies could get away with filling agent seats with mere warm bodies. Today's agents must be able to handle complex call transactions and customer email as well as web-based contacts support high-end customer accounts and participate in numerous important off-phone projects.

So then why are so many companies paying today's agents yesterday's wages?

"Call center agents aren't paid nearly what they deserve. They have one of the toughest and most important jobs in the company, though make less than employees who have positions that are less stressful and require fewer skills," says a call center manager for a bank in Texas.

She's not the only one who feels this way. We have spoken with several call center managers and consultants who think that companies aren't backing up their claims about the value of the call center with adequate compensation for frontline staff—particularly those in non-sales roles.

Companies Ignore Customer Service Agents' Impact on Revenue

"It often takes an edict of God to get a salary increase for customer service agents in most call centers," says Laura Sikorski, managing partner of Sikorski-Tuerpe & Associates—a call center consulting firm in Centerport, N.Y. "Most companies still feel that the customer service agent position is at the low end of the spectrum, just an entry-level position. They don't realize the impact these agents have on revenue." Sikorski points out that a sales rep may bring in new customers with a sale, but it's the support provided by the customer service agent that so often creates customer loyalty and repeat business. "I'm not saying that sales reps don't deserve the good money that they make, I'm saying that management needs to realize the important role that dedicated customer service agents play, and pay them accordingly," says Sikorski.

Few are as impassioned over inadequate agent compensation as Mary Beth Ingram, president of the call center training consultancy Phone Pro (see her article, "A Candid Conversation on Call Center Compensation," later in this chapter).

"As the role of the call center has evolved, the job classification and resulting pay scale of the frontline staff—the people who we ask to know the most in the call center—has lagged behind," says Ingram. "I believe that wages for call center agents are woefully low and must be re-evaluated."

Ingram alludes to a study conducted by the Society of Consumer Affairs Professionals in Business (SOCAP) in 1997 to support her claims that customer service agents deserve better compensation. According to the executive summary of SOCAP's *Consumer Loyalty Study*, call centers "not only excel in delivering service quality, but are significantly affecting the consumer's future buying patterns." (Ingram explains that consumer affairs call centers are typical of many customer service centers—they handle mostly compliment, complaint and inquiry calls from existing or prospective customers.) Specifically, the study revealed that the typical consumer affairs agent contributed an average of $1,359,745 per year of what SOCAP refers to as "lifetime consumer loyalty dollars." The value of a typical phone call from a customer to a consumer affairs call center was found to be $95.

Ingram points out that many consumer affairs calls are about small-end products like toothpaste, food items, etc., and that, therefore, $95 is probably a low figure for call centers that support higher-end goods and services (computers, banks, etc). Even still, she gladly uses the figure uncovered by the SOCAP study in her calculations.

"Say your typical agent handles 50 calls a day—a conservative number," says Ingram. "That agent handles $4,750 ($95 x 50) a day for the company. In a week, the agent handles $23,750. In a year, $1,235,000! And we all know that it's not uncommon for agents in many call centers to handle 100 calls a day or more. The point is that the amount of loyalty dollars to which frontline staff contribute is astounding, but these figures are overlooked by most senior managers."

Given these numbers, how much should a qualified customer service agent be paid? Ingram's response: a wage/salary more comparable to that of sales staff. To get a rough idea of what this might be, she suggests taking the $1,235,000 figure previously mentioned to determine how much of that a typical outside sales rep would be paid. Average commission for sales reps is about 5 percent, meaning that they would receive $61,750 a year. "Even if we give experienced customer service agents only 3 percent commission," Ingram explains, "they would still be making more than $37,000 a year. That's a darn sight better than the $17,000 to $20,000 that most are making now."

Like Sikorski, Ingram isn't trying to reduce sales reps' salaries. "I don't have a problem with sales staff making a lot of money—they work hard to earn it. But let's pay the customer service folks—the people who are in the position to ensure years of repeat business—what they are truly worth, too."

Poor Payment = High Turnover

The most damaging effect of inadequate agent compensation is the high employee turnover so many call centers experience. While many managers acknowledge that low pay isn't the only cause of attrition, they claim it is the reason most commonly cited by agents leaving the center. At many call centers, agents even make lateral moves to what managers say are less-challenging though higher-paying jobs in other departments within the company.

"During exit interviews, agents often tell us, 'Hey, I'm taking a promotion for an easier job in the company,'" says the Texas bank center manager cited previously. While frustrated by the attrition, she says she can't blame the employees. "Why should an agent want to work his or her heart out in the call center for $8 or $9 an hour if he or she can work in a department that is less stressful, provides similar opportunities for advancement and pays $11 an hour?"

Basing agent pay on what benchmarking results and salary guides suggest is not a solution to the problem of poor agent compensation, she adds. If the majority of companies don't pay agents what they are worth, why mimic them?

[35]

"I've been to several meetings with managers of other bank call centers where we discuss numerous issues—particularly compensation—for benchmarking purposes," she says. "But the problem is that none of our companies are paying agents what they deserve. I've told colleagues at these meetings, 'Unless some of us get agent pay up, we're all going to be stuck in this benchmarking loop and continue to underpay agents, which will cause high turnover to continue.'"

In addition to causing existing agents to flee, the mediocre pay at many call centers makes it difficult to attract qualified applicants to replace them, leading to poor service and even more turnover. The resulting high cost of training and retraining agents should alone be enough to compel senior management to increase frontline wages, says the bank manager, but management just writes high turnover off as a necessary cost of having a call center.

What is most frustrating to her is that management doesn't understand how essential agents are to the overall financial success of the organization. Regardless of whether or not they are involved in selling, agents at the bank have their fingers on the pulse of much of the company's revenue every day, says the manager, and their compensation should reflect that.

"Agents have a crucial, valuable job. They need to know a tremendous amount of information and are responsible for providing excellent service to retain highly valuable credit card accounts. But without offering decent pay, it's hard to find and/or hold on to the kind of people who can do those things well."

Rather than just complain about the compensation/turnover problems at her call center, the manager is currently reviewing them with senior management at the bank. "We are raising awareness about the value of agents and the cost of turnover, which will hopefully lead to positive change."

Agents Still Viewed as "Operators" at Financial Service Call Centers, Says Manager

Andrew Pohlmann, call center manager for Old Kent Financial Corp. in Grand Rapids, Mich., agrees that customer service agents' crucial role in customer and profit retention is underplayed, and says they are underpaid as a result. "Most financial services call centers originated from backroom operational areas," he says. "It's difficult for management to take the leap and say that customer service agents are no longer operations workers, they are customer contact workers who are in the trenches and are as important to revenue as the frontline sales reps. Instead, customer service agents are still viewed as 'operators' and paid accordingly."

Convincing senior management to increase customer service agents' pay is a challenge because management wants to see clear-cut data on revenue generated by those agents, says Pohlmann. While information like that revealed by SOCAP's Consumer Loyalty Study can help in this regard, tying customer service agent performance directly to revenue retention/gains for senior management to see is difficult. But that doesn't mean that call center managers should throw in the towel.

"You need to do everything you can to impress upon senior management that customer service agents are valuable assets, not liabilities," says Pohlmann. "It isn't easy, but you need to try to break it down to dollars and cents and say, 'This is how much we pay agents now; this is how many transactions they conduct; this is what a typical customer relationship is worth, and this is what it costs to retain that relationship." Presenting that type of data can help you convince management to "do the right thing" and increase salaries, he says.

While it may be easier to link revenue gains to sales agent performance than to customer service agent performance, that doesn't necessarily mean that call center sales agents are paid what they deserve either, says Pohlmann. "Our sales agent compensation is pretty good, but I think they should get paid more considering the revenue they generate." He points out that sales agents in the call center are paid roughly the same as sales people in the bank branches, despite the fact that end-of-the-year reports show that call center sales agents generate three to four times more revenue than those in the branches.

Not an Enticing Career Move

Bank call center managers aren't the only managers frustrated by unfair agent compensation. For example, a group of seven managers/supervisors at a recent small group forum were asked, "If you were an agent, would you want to work in your call center?" Five said "no." When asked why, the primary reason given was "inadequate compensation for the work done."

Paying agents what they are worth would not only attract qualified agents to the center and retain them longer, it would encourage those with a passion for the work to make a true career out of being an agent, says one manager of a telecommunications call center.

"Not everybody wants to become a manager or executive at the company. There are many employees who would love to make being a customer service agent a career if they could make a decent living doing so. So why not make that an option and pay 'stars' a premium? Just think of the power of the call center's front line if among it were agents who loved what they do and were truly dedicated to providing the best possible service they can. But the way they are paid now, they can't look at it as a career, just as a job."

Pizza Parties Don't Pay the Piper

As important as it is to fight for fair agent compensation, consultant Sikorski warns that pay alone doesn't ensure service quality, high employee morale and low turnover.

"You still need to use creative rewards and recognition, and involve agents in interesting projects to avoid burnout," she says. "Agents need some fun injected into their often-repetitive jobs and want to know that their input is valued by the company."

But Sikorski is quick to point out that such motivational tactics often aren't enough to keep agents striving to dazzle customers. Good financial compensation needs to be worked into the mix. "You can have as many pizza parties as you want," she says, "but after awhile agents are going to want to see their performance reflected in their paychecks."

Getting senior management to change its tune on agent compensation won't happen overnight. Call center professionals must continue to demonstrate the influence their frontline staff has on customer loyalty and revenue generation/retention. The answer to "what should we pay our agents?" should not be determined by merely looking outside at what other companies are doing; the focus should be internal, based on what your agents are worth to your company.

Agent Compensation: Motivating Staff without Burying Budgets

by Dan Coen

Unlike professional athletes, even superstar call center agents are unlikely to go on strike if given the option. However, the needs that drive pro athletes are not any different than the needs that motivate agents to perform at their very best. Agents recognize the same basic tenet of compensation as athletes: Money drives performance, and performance is expected to drive money. Agents expect to receive quality compensation for quality work. While they don't expect to be paid like star baseball players, they do expect to be rewarded fairly and consistently based on fair market value.

Designing a compensation plan for call center agents can be tricky. Pay is the most critical element because it drives stability and performance. Yet pay is not the only component of a successful compensation plan for agents. Incentives and time-off often play a part in compensation plans that succeed long term. Team vs. individual bonuses and base salary vs. commission should be explored, too. Agents claim that without such elements, management doesn't make compensation exciting, and thus fails to turn it into a source of motivation.

The Principles of Agent Compensation

In my experience, I have found that there are seven principles that should be considered when implementing an effective agent compensation plan.

1. The compensation plan must be centered upon a company's ability to pay. Every company is different when assigning a certain percentage of pay to its agents. An independent customer service call center may not provide the same type of compensation agreement that a Fortune 500 firm will. Management must be cognizant of how much money and investment the company can make in the call center.

2. The compensation plan must be centered upon demand. Developing a compensation plan in the heart of a large city is quite different from coordinating a plan for a small-town call center. Many part-time agents located in small college towns are typically available only seven months out of a year, with little competition for their services. They receive an hourly wage and incentives if applicable. Full-time employees in major cities are available 12 months a year, but competition from other employers is steep. They usually receive a package that includes base salary and incentives based on company performance, if applicable. If management in a small town changes their compensation plan based on each season, they may risk alienating part-time agents who wish to work all 12 months. Similarly, continuous compensation adjustments in a major city may cause retention to suffer.

3. The compensation plan must be centered upon job requirements. While the basic concept of an agent position is the same, the job duties are always different. This means that management cannot mimic other compensation plans because each company has different objectives. A compensation plan must be centered on the objectives of each particular job. Issues to consider include, "What skills does an agent use on a daily basis?" "How does this role differ from other roles in the organization? "What type of candidates are we looking to attract?"

4. The bond between management and agent must be based on trust. The more confusion about pay, the weaker the bond. Agents feel entitled to show a lack of commitment if management flip-flops on compensation issues. They feel a loss of confidence in their superiors, all of which leads to higher turnover. If the objective of management when designing a call center compensation plan is to discourage turnover and enhance the relationship between agent and manager, the plan must be developed correctly the first time, and implemented with a long-term approach in mind.

5. A compensation agreement must be based on appropriate performance objectives. Managers may pay their agents based primarily on one or two objectives, only to learn that other objectives are more critical to the call center's success. If an established agreement leaves open any doubt about measurements or objectives, the compensation plan will falter. For example, a sales-oriented call center should compensate agents more for sales production than for overall agent availability.

6. Pay agents based on what you want them to make, regardless of industry averages. Managers may base their formulas on published compensation tables in trade magazines and newsletters. This is a mistake. If an agent accepts a position at $7.50 per hour and a monthly team bonus, then the agent assumes this is how compensation for that job works. Just because a compensation table portrays paying a part-time, inbound agent X amount per hour doesn't mean your agents may not accept something less—or demand more. I encourage management to create their standards for a position. The needs of one company may not work for another.

7. **Don't be afraid to play with BIG NUMBERS or create unique standards.** This opens the door to creative compensation. For example, suppose 100 full-time agents in your call center earn $9 per hour. What if you paid them $8 per hour? What if you took the savings ($800 per day, $4,000 per week, $16,000 every month) and applied it to measurements that could reward every agent with far more then their basic $9 each hour? To illustrate, suppose the most important objective in your call center is available time. At the moment, 30 percent of your agents have available time of between 75 percent to 100 percent. Budget the $16,000 you saved for 50 percent of agents to meet the goal of available time between 75 percent to 100 percent. If 50 percent of agents meet their goal next month, they each get a $320 bonus, which is $160 more than they would have received if they had their basic compensation plan of $9 per hour. If only 40 percent of agents meet the goal, then there is even more money to go around ($400 per agent), or more money to spend next month. Management now has created a compensation plan that rewards call center agents for doing what they are required to do anyhow. This plan excites agents to meet objectives that must be met. Agents feel motivated when presented the opportunity to strive for something unique.

Agent Input Is Essential

Merely following these seven principles is not enough; you must find out what agents want to secure a comprehensive compensation plan. Conduct focus groups with agents to get their input. The alternative to not asking for agent feedback is to develop a plan that falls short of doing what you need it to do.

Develop a survey that asks agents various questions on compensation. Keep in mind that questions like: "Would you like a higher base salary?" won't tell you anything.

Instead, try questions like:

- "Would you take a smaller base salary to possibly earn more compensation in bonuses, commissions and incentives?"
- "Is it important to you that management provides consistent prizes, awards and incentives to complement a compensation plan?"
- "Would team bonuses and bonuses in addition to your salary based upon measured goals motivate you less than a simple compensation plan that relies on individual performance?"

Creative Compensation: A Delicate Balance

Call center managers face several obstacles when designing an effective compensation plan. They must ensure that agents are compensated fairly for their work without exceeding budgets. They must also ensure that agents feel continually motivated to perform at a high level.

Too many managers stay within safe confines when developing compensation plans. While this may ensure fairness, it often limits opportunity and excitement. However, some managers become so involved with creativity and opportunity that they fail to develop a plan that produces measurable results. By developing a well-founded and inspiring compensation agreement that serves specific objectives, agents become a partner in ensuring success for your company.

Skills-Based Pay Program Raises Performance and Lowers Costs

by Julia Mayben

Who says money doesn't motivate? Not Pitney Bowes' Mailing Systems Division whose skills-based pay program has helped to significantly improve agent performance while lowering transaction costs.

The program, which was rolled out in April 1996 at the division's five call centers located throughout the U.S., has radically altered how agents' base pay is calculated. In the past, agent compensation was tied to tenure. Now salary increases are based on continuous learning and consistent performance.

"For years, we relied on the merit system, telling associates, 'If you've been at the center for a while, have kept your nose clean and, for the most part, have met your objectives, you will probably get a raise,'" recalls Jerry Terrell, director of call center operations for the Mailing Systems Division. "With the new program, we reward associates [with additional compensation] for learning additional skills and doing a good job."

Once agents are trained on a new skill, they must pass a certification test to demonstrate proficiency in that new skill. For each new skill acquired, agents receive an increase in their base pay.

When the skills-based pay program began, management also introduced a reward system for agents. Under the system, which is indirectly tied to the skills-based pay program, agents can earn quarterly bonuses of up to 15 percent of their base salary if centerwide and individual performance goals are met.

A Move Toward Multiskilled Agents

Moving away from the merit system, management set the stage for creating a more skilled workforce. As Terrell explains, "We opted to make the change because the merit program didn't drive people to learn other skills. Since our work changes, we need that flexibility. We needed a program that encouraged our associates to be multiskilled so they could move easily among different types of work as needed."

Developing the skills-based pay program was no easy task. The project involved input from many people: agents and managers in the five call center sites; representatives from the company's human resources and compensation departments; and outside consultants. The plan took 14 months to develop. "We created a whole new program vs. simply modifying the old [merit system]," explains Terrell.

Once the details were finalized, Terrell and his managers reviewed the program with call center personnel during a series of one-on-one meetings prior to officially launching it. Terrell encountered some resistance from agents who were in a "skills gap." As he explains, "About a third of the associates in the centers were long-tenured people who had been getting automatic raises for years. With the new program, the skills we were willing to pay for and the skills they had didn't match up. They were making more than what the skills-based pay plan said they could."

While a few of those people caught in the gap left the center soon after the program was launched, many others opted to work with team leaders and trainers to close their skill gaps and maintain their salaries. Most of those reps were able to catch up within 18 months, says Terrell.

Training, Certification and Cash

The skills-based pay program features nearly 50 skill blocks, which are divided into three categories: core, advanced and expert (see table on page 47). The core skill blocks include the most basic skills that agents need to acquire, with the advanced and expert skill blocks including the more complex skill bases. Within each category, there are two subgroups of skills: technical and non-technical.

Acquiring a specific skill involves a two step process: 1) training, and 2) certification. The skills training includes classroom and on-the-job instruction, which can last anywhere from two days to two weeks. The trainers at the five centers lead non-technical training, but team leaders—who are experienced agents—lead the classroom training and coaching on more complex skill blocks. "We found that the team leaders were better teachers because they knew the processes better than the trainers," says Terrell.

As part of the training process, agents must show they can effectively use each skill by completing specific proficiency requirements. The proficiency requirements vary with each skill block. In general, agents demonstrate skill proficiency by handling a set number of calls or completing tasks related to that skill, which can be observed via silent and side-by-side monitoring.

Within two weeks of completing the proficiency requirements, reps take a written certification test on the skill block. Once they pass that test, agents are deemed "certified" in that skill.

Agents earn credits after successfully completing the training/certification process for a particular skill block. Each skill block is worth one to 12 credits, depending on its complexity. Agents can then redeem the credits, which have a specific dollar value that is added to their base salary.

If an agent fails the written test, he or she is given two more chances during the following eight weeks to pass the test. If he or she fails on both attempts, he or she must start the learning process over, beginning with the classroom training.

The training department uses software that can keep track of the skills certifications for the more than 600 agents at the five Pitney Bowes call centers. The department—with input from Terrell, center managers and the scheduling team—determines what skills training should be offered and when. First, they put together a training plan for agents based on the skills needed in the call centers. Then the group works with the forecasting and scheduling team to develop a training timetable. Every timetable includes different skill-block training.

Once published, the training agenda often spawns "healthy competition" among agents, says Diane Byrum, a trainer in the Norfolk, Va., call center. "We might get four or five applicants for each skill we post. People thrive on the competition to learn new skills," explains Byrum.

Extra Effort Paying Off in Dollars and Sensational Service

The skills-based pay program requires constant maintenance. Much of the managers' time is now spent reviewing training requirements and skill proficiencies. "The merit system didn't require much of the manager's time," says Terrell. "With this program, managers have to monitor things like how skills are grouped. As we get more efficient, we have to look at realigning the skills. The skills that weighed in as important before might not be as important later."

But the extra work is worth it, providing more multiskilled agents in the call centers, adds Terrell. The centers are now able to adjust the workforce as needed to meet service level goals. Today, the five centers are regularly achieving their new service level target of answering 90 percent of the calls in 30 seconds, up from the previous average of 80/30.

Better agent performance has also enabled the centers to reduce their transaction costs. Since the skills-based pay program was implemented, transaction costs have dropped 11 percent. "The pay program has made associates want to take responsibility for their job and be more efficient," says Terrell. "We've become a high-performance organization."

Agents are happier with their jobs because of the skills-based pay program. One reason for this is that agents feel their salary reviews are more objective. "The skills-based pay program has eliminated rep complaints about favoritism," says Terrell. "It's well-defined; everyone knows how it works and what they have to do to increase their pay."

Gloria Privott, a team leader at the Norfolk center, adds that agents like the ability to "move around, learn new things and make more money. That's what keeps associates here and performing their jobs well."

Joni Ashley, an agent at Pitney Bowes' call center in Spokane, Wash., agrees.

"We have more control over our future now," says Ashley. "We can take training, upgrade our skills and take a test to prove we are up to speed. If you know the plan up front and you know there are opportunities, you're more inclined to stay with the company."

Chapter 2

Pitney Bowes Skills-Based Pay "Blocks"

Non-technical Skills	Technical Skills
Core	**Core**

Non-technical Skills

Core

(Required)
- Orientation
- Telephone skills
- Group/interpersonal dynamics
- Computer system
- Company/product knowledge
- Phone system
- Meter security

Advanced
- Planning and decision making
- Group/team dynamics
- Cycle time
- Instructional training

Expert
- Feedback
- Problem solving
- Effective communication
- Faciliation skills
- Team dynamics
- Quality tools
- Instructional training
- Data analysis

Technical Skills

Core
- Postage by phone
- Order processing
- Equipment move and track
- Rapid response overflow
- Lease maintenance
- Rate change
- Retention program
- Sales information

Advanced
- Order processing
- Rapid response overflow
- Equipment move and track
- Service support
- Account resolution
- Account maintenance
- Inbound billing
- Lease maintenance
- Postange by phone
- Retention program

Expert
- Account resolution
- Inbound billing/sales info
- Service support
- Rapid response performance
- Staffing analysis
- Postage by phone

Chapter 2

A Candid Conversation on Call Center Compensation

Mary Beth Ingram is president and founder of Phone Pro, an Indianapolis-based call center consulting firm that specializes in providing soft skills training for frontline staff. As a speaker, she is a perennial favorite at call center conferences, including the World Conference on Incoming Call Center Management.

Question: Whom do we ask to know the most, but often pay the least in the call center?

Answer: The frontline staff.

What you are about to read is a personal perspective on phone rep compensation. It is based on 12 years of observations in more than 100 call centers spanning a wide variety of industries and applications. It is my own view. Some will agree with it. Others will take issue with it.

Compensation is a touchy, sensitive issue. There are wonderful exceptions to cite where compensation is commensurate with the requirements and talents of the staff. For example, my hat goes off to the consumer affairs profession that, in my opinion, leads the way in fair compensation for call center professionals. But even this accolade is not 100-percent true for all consumer affairs applications.

As a trainer and consultant, I have had the privilege of working in small to gargantuan call centers—small, as in fewer than 10 reps; gargantuan, as in 1,400 reps. The industries vary from a scientific research help desk to a moving company dispatching center; from healthcare and insurance customer service to consumer debt collections; from order entry for footwear, to computer technology hotlines; from utility companies to car companies; from consumer affairs for beverages to consumer affairs for household cleaning products. The calls range from the simple to the complex; from less than a minute in talk time to 20 minutes in problem-solving time. The callers are from the broadest spectrum you can imagine, with questions and concerns that run the gamut of trivial to critical. This is the broad base from which come my observations on rep compensation.

Chapter 2

Rep Pay Scale Lagging Behind in Evolving Industry

When you look at the evolution of the call center, you see tremendous and positive change. The roots of the call center go back to the "plain vanilla customer service department" of the 1960s and 1970s. This was first and foremost a support function. Its primary mission was administrative tasks with a secondary mission to answer the phone. Customer service representative, secretary, file clerk and order entry clerk were the titles you found there. Contact between the customer and the company was mostly through the outside salesperson, and the consumer was not yet much of a player.

The power of the consumer developed in the '70s, built steam in the '80s and exploded into a force to be reckoned with in the '90s! As this has occurred, the plain vanilla customer service department has given way to the call center. Now there is often a call center for consumer affairs and one for customer service; one for new accounts and one for collections; one for the help desk and one for dispatch. Call loads continue to grow. Technology advances. The primary mission of a call center is to answer the phone to serve the customer or consumer, and the secondary mission is to do administrative tasks (now mostly PC-driven). That's a complete flip from where the industry began.

The call center has become the pulse of the organization, the corporate service center, the nerve center, the one-stop shop dream! How envious sales, marketing, communications, public relations and other departments have become of its resources, talents and access to the buyer. Many call centers are profit centers and are adding revenue to the corporate balance sheet.

But as the role of the call center has grown and evolved, the job classification and resulting pay scale of the staff has lagged behind.

I'm Willing to Be the Renegade!

I believe that, in most organizations, wages for call center reps are woefully low and need to be reevaluated. This includes taking a look at incentive programs, which are sometimes used not to enhance and increase someone's earnings (although that's how the program is sold), but to keep wages artificially depressed through a set of questionable, usually subjective, standards.

Think about what call center reps can do. In most centers, they are skilled at operating multiple computer programs, many of them custom applications. Reps are able to read and assimilate instantaneous packets of data from the computer about buying history, demographics, account numbers, history of past conversations, alerts for credit problems—all while conversing coherently on the phone.

Reps take in a constant stream of information from reader boards on current ACD stats, not to mention messages flashed about the special of the day, reminders to cross-sell and upsell, items in back-order status, items overstocked that need to be moved at discount. Reps interact with a wide spectrum of callers from either the consumer or the customer side of the business. They possess an excellent working knowledge of company products or services. They maintain a firm grasp of company knowledge as it applies to procedures and policies. They know the organization well enough to gather appropriate resources for the customer and to serve as their advocates. Many are proficient in current promotional activity, support outside sales representatives, and even manage entire territories in some instances. They interact with marketing, credit and shipping, and are active participants in call center project teams, all the while completing the administrative and followup work necessary to satisfy the consumer or customer and the boss! Outside salespeople often are not as well-versed and resource-ready as the average call center rep.

Your list of rep "duties" may be less or it may be more in your call center. Now look at your requirements for a position in your center. Have they stayed the same or are they getting tougher? The days of "must like to talk on the phone" as a job requirement have often given way to "must have a college degree."

And what is the average compensation for call center staff? Surveys abound. Information can be skewed and of limited value based on whom and how many responded. But hourly wages yield, on average and without commissions, a low of $13,460 a year for a full-time job. The salaried position fares better at just $20,000 a year (for 1997).

The Paradox of Incentives

What about incentive programs? When tied to sales productivity, incentives can be great and success is easy to track. When the measure is more illusive, incentives can be demoralizing. I witnessed a rep get "scored" low because the coach determined the rep did not offer enough options in the call. Never mind that the rep sold the caller the product quickly and effectively with the first option presented. That coach's determination cost that rep $1 per hour for a 40-hour week on an hourly wage of $6.50. Scoring is always objective in the real world: baseball, hockey, golf, bridge tournaments. Isn't scoring low in a subjective environment really "opinioning" low? Anyone who is serious about coaching and interested in the personal development of his or her staff knows intimately how fine the line is.

What about incentives for stats (e.g., goals for number of calls taken, talk time, after-call work, availability)? At a glance, these incentives seem logical. What if you get the luck of the draw and the ACD decides to send you all the problem-resolution calls and your neighbor gets simple orders or inquiries? What if you are asked to participate in a meeting or must troubleshoot a situation for a customer with the marketing department? What happens when the balance of quality and quantity is affected by the drive for 50 cents more per hour on your paycheck? And if management makes allowances for all the special circumstances, who gets the tedious job of tracking it all when they could be supporting the frontline staff or talking with escalated callers?

Outsourcing Creating "Third World Wage" Strata?

Early on I stated that the consumer affairs industry is often the exception in this area. It has led in the compensation game with higher earnings and salaried positions. But outsourcing is changing the landscape for consumer affairs as well as other call center applications.

Far too many frontline staff at outsourcing companies are paid in the $6 per hour range. A conversation I had not too long ago with someone working at an outsourcing company revealed he had just secured his position at $7 per hour, which was 50 cents higher than the outsourcing firm he worked for across town. He had a college degree, was married with one child and held another job to make a living. His call center job required him to be proficient in computer technology and Internet software.

And yet, outsourcing is not a "cheap alternative." That's not why a company chooses to go outside. The decision is more complex, more strategic and, in fact, a major expense item. My fear is that the frontline job in outsourcing is creating a sort of "third world wage" strata.

Check Should Reflect Respect

Well, what's the bottom line? I simply desire to see the call center profession garner more respect, not just in verbal and written appreciation of what the call center means to the company, but in the paychecks of the folks who make it happen, who are asked to be the first voice and image, who are required to be trained and knowledgeable, who encounter the best and the worst of humanity on a daily basis, who are probably in the call center because their desire to serve is their strongest trait. Perhaps for one day, just one day, all call center frontline staff should stay at home. Count the lost revenue from sales and the cost of lost good will. Then get the executives down to the call center to answer the phones, and we may just find the budget for wages and salaries increased to reflect the talent and skill required for the job.

Chapter 2

Chapter 3:
Incentives

Use Incentive Programs to Link Desired Behaviors with Rewards

Air Canada's Agent-Run Incentive Program Flying High

Incentives that Rev Up and Retain Agents

Use Incentive Programs to Link Desired Behaviors with Rewards

by Leslie Hansen Harps

Incentive programs "are intended to link the behavior of individual employees to the types of performance that you need in the organization," observes Gerry Ledford, practice manager of employee performance and rewards for Nextera's Sibson Consulting Group in Los Angeles. Incentive programs in some call centers achieve only lukewarm results or, worse, backfire and reinforce the wrong kind of behavior, while others exceed expectations.

"Incentive programs that are aligned with customer satisfaction, have clearly identified performance standards and are consistent" can work very well in the call center, says Anne Nickerson, principal of Call Center Coach, Ellington, Conn. She cites a successful call center incentive program in a highly complex financial industry in which the goal was to improve the accuracy of information given to customers. When the incentive program was implemented, all the necessary tools were put into place, including clear standards and expectations, a system that provided accurate information, training and "mini-trainings" for the call center agents, and a monitoring and coaching process. Reps who performed well became peer coaches and all coaches were trained and calibrated to ensure consistency in their evaluation.

Unfortunately, many call center incentive programs "tend not to be very well-implemented and often are not very well-designed," Ledford says. Probably the single most common problem of design, he says, is failure to use a broad enough measurement base. "You need a balance of measures to reflect the different kinds of performance you want from people. Otherwise, you'll sub-optimize."

Design an incentive program that rewards productivity only, such as handling more calls in an hour, and your service quality may suffer. But if you incent only quality, Ledford says, "you almost certainly will see productivity decline."

A well-designed, well-implemented incentive program may have as many as three to five variables, or even more, he says. Finding the right mix and balance is one of the keys to a successful program.

Chapter 3

Broadening Measures

Boston Coach, an executive sedan service, revamped its incentive program to increase the number of measures, reports Nancy Leeser, vice president of international reservations and customer service for the Boston-based company. "When we first introduced the incentive program," she explains, "it was based purely on quality," measuring number of errors per transaction. CSRs who met their goal received an incentive of 5 percent of their salary. The program was deemed to be too subjective, and "we weren't sure we were getting our money's worth," Leeser says.

A supervisor in the call center worked with CSRs to develop a revised incentive program through which reps can earn up to 5 percent of their salary. "It's a multi-faceted program," Leeser says. To determine the categories, "we selected the things that were important to us in running the business." Reps earn points in the following categories:

- Individual attendance and punctuality.
- Schedule adherence.
- Number of transactions.
- Level reached in the company's career pathing program (with number of points awarded increasing as the level increases).
- Improvements in number of service failures for the center as a whole.

Depending upon overall point total, a CSR can earn a 100 percent payout, a 50 percent payout—or no payout at all.

"We are getting what we hoped for" from the program, says Leeser. Implemented last year, the program was fine-tuned this year, combining attendance and punctuality into one category and moving to a quality measure that rewards group, rather than individual, performance.

Rewarding with Recognition

In addition to its corporate-wide recognition programs, the service area of Independence Blue Cross (IBC) uses a multifaceted recognition program called "Blue Diamond."

"It's a monthly program that recognizes our service reps," explains Hank Kearney, senior director of member service for the Philadelphia-based company. The program keys in on four areas:

- Attendance and punctuality.
- Accuracy and professionalism, as determined through monitoring (reps must receive a rating of 99.5 percent or more).
- Performing at "expectations-plus" in categories such as staff time, after-call work and follow-up work.
- Going above and beyond the call of duty.

Contributions in the last category are noted by a rep's supervisor, says Roe Tabasco, manager of quality assurance and training for IBC. For example, a rep may have helped to train others within the unit, handled special projects with timeliness and accuracy, worked overtime, received complimentary letters from members, made suggestions for improving work operations or simply may have been an enthusiastic, motivated coworker.

Blue Diamond awards are given out on the last Friday of each month on "Blue Diamond Day." Reps who have earned a Blue Diamond receive a certificate, a blue diamond to put on the certificate and a gift voucher for the company cafeteria. The number of individuals who receive Blue Diamonds varies, with perhaps 10 to 20 of the 225 service reps at the call center recognized each month.

Once a year, a recognition breakfast is held for the top Blue Diamond winners. These employees receive a certificate, an American Express gift certificate and a gold coin (part of the company's corporate-wide recognition program).

The program has been in place for more than five years and is very successful, Kearney says, especially with reps who are making the call center their career.

Balance Service and Productivity

When developing an incentive program, suggests Gerry Ledford, first define what role the call center plays, then identify key measures that support the role. This will enable you to tie rewards for the individual to the type of performance you want from the call center. For example, "if you don't see the call center as a sales channel to reach customers and expand the business, then rewarding cross-selling is a waste of time," he says.

Use a balanced mix of metrics, Ledford advises. For example, a productivity measure, such as number of calls per hour could be balanced with a metric from customer satisfaction surveys or measures of individual quality. It's crucial not to reward productivity at the expense of service quality, and vice versa.

"Productivity is a lot easier to measure than quality," according to Nancy Leeser. "You have to put your money where your mouth is on the quality piece, going out of your way to reward quality." Boston Coach does not include "number of phone calls handled" in its incentive program, she says. "We reward things which lead to that—if you're in your seat adhering to your schedule, you will take more phone calls. But we've never given a target number of calls reps need to take in a day."

Independence Blue Cross intentionally does not include a productivity category in its recognition program. "We want to send the message that we'd rather have it done right the first time, so we do not emphasize the reps having to take a certain number of calls, or having a certain average talk time," says Hank Kearney. "I'd rather have a rep with a higher talk time who delivers quality service—one who's leaving customers "wowed"—than a rep who moves customers in and out quickly."

A Learning Opportunity

For an incentive program to change behavior, it's important to combine it with coaching—particularly when it comes to service quality, says Anne Nickerson. She describes an ideal incentive program as one that has "clear, consistent rewards tied to improvement in behavior, with opportunities for everyone to understand and learn what that behavior is and looks like."

This would include giving call center agents feedback immediately after a call and letting them know what they can do to improve their score, as well as their management of the customer. "Deliver the feedback in a way that's very specific," Nickerson advises. "Give examples, models and approaches that the person can use" to improve his or her performance.

An incentive program combined with coaching will get better results, agrees Gerry Ledford. "People tend to act as if you can announce an incentive plan, turn on the switch and it will work. That's not the case. You have to do all the hard management labor of communicating, training, reinforcing, monitoring and coaching" to get the results you want.

"It's quite possible to get unintended results, to unintentionally reinforce behaviors you don't want," he says, so it's critical to monitor the incentive program to make sure you're getting the results you expected.

What Type of Reward?

"All things being equal, dollars are going to be more effective than praise" as a reward, according to Ledford. "While different things have different reward value for individuals, almost anybody is going to find money motivating." The question is, how much money does it take to drive a change in behavior?

"The available evidence suggests that an incentive becomes powerful when it represents 5 percent to 10 percent of base pay," Ledford says

"Money is one incentive, but there are many more," observes Anne Nickerson. "I also see incentives that are fun, which helps improve morale." At one call center, for example, agents who earned a certain number of points could put leaves on the branch of a tree. Each completed branch was worth so many points, which could be turned in for rewards such as massages, manicures and pedicures, free pizza and certificates at the local mall. Agents loved the program and the prizes.

At a health care and financial services call center, Nickerson says, when agents met and maintained a specified quality goal, managers would make and serve breakfast or serve reps an afternoon treat from a fully equipped snack cart. In another call center, an entire team that cleaned up a database earned a trip to Las Vegas by "beating the clock."

Whatever reward you decide to use in your incentive program, remember that "the more often you reward behavior, the more often you'll get it," Ledford says. Monthly or quarterly incentive programs are the most common. If the time horizon is longer than that, the program is less likely to reinforce the behavior you're seeking. So make sure there's lots of communication and publicity to keep interest high.

Chapter 3

Are They Worth It?

Incentive programs that are designed and implemented well can pay off handsomely. Gerry Ledford cites a study conducted by the American Compensation Association. The study, which looked at 660-plus incentive plans across a range of industries, identified the net return on payout as 134 percent. "That's for an average payout of three percent," Ledford says. "Typically, the higher potential for gain, the higher the success rate." Companies in the most successful quartile in this study had a whopping net return of 378 percent.

While there have been some whopping failures, on the whole, incentive programs are quite successful, Ledford says. "And they're one of the most successful types of intervention you can come up with."

A Different Look at Incentive Programs

"To me, delivering a certain level of quality and efficiency with productivity is how you keep your job," notes Donna K. Richmond, president of the Richmond Group, a customer service consulting firm located in Wheaton, Ill. "I think that an incentive should be for above and beyond the call of duty."

Richmond has strong feelings about incentive programs in the call center. "The goals have to be a real stretch, but they also have to be reachable." She cites the case of one call center paying a base salary of $20,000, with a potential incentive payout of as much as $10,000. "But the incentive was nearly impossible to get," Richmond says. "Once the agents realized it wasn't do-able, they either quit or stopped trying."

She also suggests that managers examine whether or not they can achieve the results they desire without an incentive program. "Can you get the same or better results by paying people more money, and getting more talented, more experienced people?"

Finally, she advises, don't treat the incentive program in a vacuum. "If you're monitoring people for the program, take advantage of the opportunity to look at the whole picture." Examine the process and root out barriers that may get in the way of agents doing their jobs.

Air Canada's Agent-Run Incentive Program Flying High

by Dan Coen

When it comes to staff motivation and incentives, Air Canada's Vancouver reservations center relies on a team of proven experts—its own agents.

"A team of call center agents plans and administers all of our contests and incentives in the call center," says Butch Gregoire, manager of customer service and reservations for the Vancouver center, one of Air Canada's five reservation centers in Canada. "We felt it would bring accountability to the staff and add more fun for the agents if their own peers were involved in the coordination of our motivational efforts. Agents have their finger on the pulse of our center, so they are the natural people to create incentives for everyone."

The agent-run incentive program began in 1996 with six reservation agents comprising the Incentive Committee. Prior to the formation of the committee, morale had been good, but not energized, says Gregoire. Managers and supervisors did their best to foster enthusiasm and spirit, but their other duties hindered their ability to create an incentive-oriented environment. "Agents motivating agents" was a logical step.

Providing Peers with Inspiration and Information

The Incentive Committee's six members are dedicated to developing and promoting contests and prizes for fellow agents in the call center. All incentives are product- and knowledge-driven, helping to educate agents while inspiring them to perform.

"Our biggest challenge as a committee is identifying contests or incentives that meet three goals," explains Vanessa Goad, an agent who has been on the Incentive Committee for two years. "First, any contest must not get in the way of performing our primary job, which is providing service on the telephones. Second, everybody must be given an opportunity to participate in each contest. Third, each contest must teach our agents something new, whether that entails sales skills, product information or computer training."

Being a member of the Incentive Committee is a job all its own, says Goad, who originally joined the team to help bring some excitement to what can be a mundane job. Every two weeks the committee meets to discuss future incentives and contests and to coordinate the rules and promotion of events. They are each assigned duties, ranging from organizing prizes and awards to developing promotional materials and regulations.

To help them plan accurately for their audience of 131 reservation agents, committee members constantly encourage feedback. Questionnaires and surveys are handed out to agents twice a year, and nearly 100 percent are returned and tabulated. Using the feedback of their peers, the committee develops the various contests and incentives.

The committee receives a small amount of money from the company to help fund the various incentives. "We provide them with a limited budget," says Gregoire, "so they need to be creative when choosing prizes if they are to succeed in motivating the other agents. They have done quite well establishing relationships with hotels, restaurants, movie theaters and retail stores around Canada."

A Closer Look at Committee's Creations

One of the most successful contests the Incentive Committee created was "Victoria Day Escape." The contest, which took place during Victoria Day, the Canadian national holiday that falls on the third Monday in May, featured one very simple objective: book flights to the city of Victoria. To help motivate agents during the contest, the Incentive Committee created posters and fliers promoting the city of Victoria and posted them around the call center.

Each time an agent booked such a flight, his or her name was placed in a drawbox. Entries were unlimited and names were drawn weekly. Winners received various prizes including gift certificates to local restaurants. At the end of the three-week contest, one name was drawn for the grand prize—a two-night stay in one of the finest hotels in Victoria, airfare included.

Another successful contest created by the Incentive Committee was the "Air Canada/United Airlines Codeshare Challenge." Air Canada has a working agreement with United Airlines to service passengers looking to fly to or from cities/countries not serviced by Air Canada. The Codeshare Challenge contest was intended to enhance Air Canada agents' knowledge about United Airlines. For example, agents took quizzes on United's hubs and destinations. Agents who did well on the quizzes qualified for prizes, such as gift certificates to clothing stores and restaurants.

"This was a big tournament for our department because it lasted for weeks and met our objectives for fun and knowledge," explains Goad. "Agents particularly enjoyed it because plenty of prizes were given away." Agents also competed to generate the most revenue during the Codeshare Challenge. Prizes were awarded for things like most tickets booked for applicable cities and most electronic tickets sold.

Not all contests in the call center run on such a grand scale. For instance, the popular "Tip Box" contest rewards agents who submit the best sales skills or product information tips to help their colleagues. Winners receive gift certificates to movies, restaurants or retail outlets.

Quality and Union Issues Top List of Challenges

While the agent-run incentive program has been a big success at the Vancouver reservations center, there are some challenges. For instance, finding time for meetings can be difficult for Incentive Committee members. Because they work different schedules, the members sometimes find themselves trying to play catch-up in order to put together quality programs. "We have trouble sticking to our meetings every two weeks, so two or three of us often get together on a spur of the moment and begin planning," says Goad.

Another challenge the Incentive Committee faces is effectively working educational aspects into each contest. For example, one contest—"Sing for Your Supper"—features agent groups who sing "Oh Canada" at the front of the call center whenever they meet certain sales objectives. While this contest is fun for agents and adds levity to the daily grind, it isn't as educational as other contests, such as "How Literate Are You?" where agents write a 250-word essay using as many Air

Chapter 3

Canada terms and as much product information as possible.

Perhaps the biggest challenge Air Canada has had to overcome regarding its agent-run incentive program is the fact that the reservations center is unionized. The union initially had serious concerns about the program. "They didn't see why agents should be congratulated for doing a good job at the expense of other agents when they should all be doing a good job anyhow," Gregoire recalls.

Gregoire and his staff explained to the union that motivation and incentives are critical to call center success, and that putting agents in charge of the program was the optimum way to put together the best programs for all agents. But it wasn't until the union leaders saw the program in action that they gave their support. As Goad explains, "Once the union observed how well our contests and prizes had motivated the other agents, it became a huge supporter of what we do. The union has even talked about featuring our results in an annual newsletter that it produces for its members."

Success May Spread Enterprisewide

Due to the success of the agent-run incentive program at the Vancouver center, Air Canada is considering implementing the program enterprisewide. This would involve forming a national incentive committee of agents responsible for developing contests for all centers. "It's close to a reality," Goad explains, "but the implementation is intricate and will take some time. It's hard enough developing incentives for and motivating 131 reservation agents; on a national scale with more than 1,000 agents it would be even more complex."

Whether or not the program goes national, Gregoire knows that it will continue to help his agents excel and take pride in what they do.

"Many of our 131 agents were caught in the normalcy of the daily call center world before the Incentive Committee was formed," he says. "Now they have new life. It is quite common to hear agents who have been with the company 15 or 20 years say how much fun they are having each time they arrive to work because of the contests, incentives and prizes."

Incentives that Rev Up and Retain Agents

by Leslie Hansen Harps

Good incentive programs benefit both the employee and the organization. They can excite and energize call center agents, and improve morale, quality and performance. And they can help call centers retain their best agents—a crucial benefit in today's tight labor market.

But a poorly designed incentive program can backfire, create disgruntled employees and negatively affect service and quality. Planning and managing an incentive program begins with ensuring that it is aligned with your organization's—and your call center's—culture and mission. This means that, if you are committed to delivering top-notch service, your incentive programs should include a balance of quality and quantity components. Over-emphasizing "the numbers"—i.e., number of calls handled per shift—can cause quality and service to suffer.

It's also important to consider your incentive program through the eyes of the people it is designed to reward: your call center staff. Otherwise you may find that the very activities meant to spark productivity, service and morale may actually hamper them.

And while "soft" rewards like ice cream socials and "thank you" certificates from supervisors are important, they should comprise just one part of an overall reward and recognition program. Agents need to feel valued, and need to feel that their contributions are recognized throughout the organization—by senior management as well as by other departments.

Finally, incentive programs should reinforce and supplement solid compensation and benefits—they cannot be a substitute for them. This article assumes that agents are paid fairly and competitively.

What Do You Want the Program to Push?

Call center incentive programs can be used to:

- Reward performance or effort that has already taken place;

Chapter 3

- Motivate improvement in individual, team or call center performance; and

- Encourage change in agent behavior, such as reducing absenteeism.

Designing an effective call center incentive program begins with identifying precisely what you want your program to accomplish. Do you want to recognize individual accomplishments? Strengthen team spirit? Drive improvements in service levels or quality? Do you want to recognize performance after it occurs (via "spot" awards, for example) or spark improvement in future performance?

Whatever your specific goals and objectives, you need to make some important decisions before designing your incentive program:

1. Rewarding the few or the many. Singling out one or a handful of winners is great for those who win, but it actually can be demoralizing for the majority of agents who don't.

Consider balancing individual award programs such as "Agent of the Month" with programs that are designed to reward a larger percentage of the group. Some incentive programs are designed to make everyone a winner whenever someone

---

Respecting Differences

Effective incentive programs take into account generational, cultural and individual differences among employees. What motivates one agent may be a turn-off for another. For example, a study conducted by F-O-R-T-U-N-E Personnel Consultants studied "baby-boomers" (born between 1945-54); "baby-busters" (1955-64) and "Generation Xers" (1965-74). Each group's top reason for staying with a present employer was different:

- Opportunity for career advancement was cited by 51 percent of Generation Xers as a reason to stay (compared to 36 percent of baby-boomers and just 22 percent of baby-busters).

- The work environment was the top reason for staying put for baby-boomers.

- Work/family balance was the No. 1 reason for baby-busters.

Using a mix of rewards can help meet the needs of today's workforce. Training that leads to greater employability may be a great motivator for Generation Xers, while baby-busters might prize time off or rewards that can be used by families as well as individuals.

Source: www.towers.com

achieves a certain level of performance or completes certain tasks. An important side benefit of these programs is the sense of community and team spirit that they foster.

2. Individual vs. team. Incentive programs can be used to recognize individual or team achievements, and to spark individual or team performance improvement. There are pros and cons of each approach.

All-team programs in which everyone's contribution is recognized can de-motivate high performers who may feel that their individual accomplishments are not appreciated. All-individual programs, on the other hand, can result in excessive competition among agents that can be harmful in a team setting. That's why many incentive programs feature a blend of individual and team rewards.

3. Monetary vs. non-monetary rewards. While cash awards can be popular, evidence is mounting that cash is not always the greatest motivator. One study, conducted by the American Management Association, found that incentives which help employees improve their skills—such as technical and interpersonal skills training—were considered more effective motivators than immediate financial rewards.

According to American Express Incentive Services, "when companies try to motivate employees with an extra paycheck, the award dollars typically go toward the necessities: laundry detergent, diapers, car payments. But non-cash awards—gift certificates, debit card-type awards, travel and merchandise—leave participants with tangible reminders or fond memories of their hard work." The company cites a three-to-one return on investment in non-cash rewards compared to cash rewards.

The best way to find out what will motivate your agents the most is to ask them. This can be done using a survey (which should be anonymous) or via team or staff meetings.

Once you learn what motivates your agents and decide to incorporate non-monetary rewards in your incentive program, you can have great fun identifying potential rewards. Examples include:

- Points that can be accumulated to earn merchandise
- Fun contests (such as one modeled after the television show, "Who Wants to Be a Millionaire?" with service- and product-related questions and creative prizes)

Chapter 3

- Paid time off
- Tickets to movies, sporting events, concerts or plays
- A day at the spa
- Big-ticket consumer items, such as a television, personal computer or home entertainment center
- An all-expense-paid trip or weekend at a local hotel/resort
- Certificates, trophies, plaques
- Dinner out for two, with baby-sitting services provided as appropriate
- Special meals (such as a lobster dinner) delivered to the agent's home
- Group food functions (such as a barbecue, picnic or pizza parties)
- Celebrations (such as an awards dinner)
- Parties tied to the theme of the incentive program, such as a tailgate party

Because different things motivate different people, effective incentive programs often enable agents to select their rewards from a menu of prizes or feature a combination of cash and non-cash rewards.

Disarm De-motivators

For an incentive program to be fully effective, it's important to identify and minimize/eliminate those things that can potentially de-motivate agents.

De-motivators can range from a bleak working environment to constant time on the phones; from low rates of pay to excessive paperwork; from a slow computer system to lack of respect from senior management or poor response from an interfacing department.

What de-motivates your agents will vary from person to person. But chances are good that there are some overall things that frustrate and de-motivate nearly everyone. One way to identify them is to include a question about de-motivators when soliciting agent feedback for your incentive program. Then do something about it.

12 Steps to Develop an Effective Incentive Program

Regardless of the type of incentive program you decide to implement, follow these 12 steps to make sure that it motivates and energizes agents and gets the results that you seek:

1. Identify goals and objectives of the incentive program.

2. Put together a team that will plan and design the program.

3. Develop the planning process and schedule.

4. Identify budget for the year.

5. Review previous reward and recognition efforts, and research other call centers' experiences.

6. **Seek employee feedback through team or staff meetings, focus groups and confidential surveys.** Find out what motivates the greatest number of people, and what the de-motivators are.

7. **Design the program so that it meets your goals and objectives.** What will the criteria include? Should it reward individual and/or team performance? Will it be inclusive or selective? How will potential equity and popularity contest issues be addressed? What will be the process for nomination and selection? How will the awards be distributed? Get professional advice on any tax and legal issues.

8. **Test it out to make sure that it will get the results you seek.** Solicit feedback from agents, team leaders and supervisors. View it through the eyes of the employees who will participate in the program.

9. **Revise the program as necessary.**

10. **Develop a communications strategy that covers how you will announce the program, maintain interest, announce the winners, etc.** Put together supporting materials, including answers to frequently asked questions.

11. **Roll out the program.** Watch it carefully. Try to keep interest up throughout the program. If participation lags, find out why.

12. **Evaluate results.** Did you get the results you expected? If not, why not? Seek agent feedback: What did they like, what didn't they like? Incorporate these findings in your next incentive program.

Inspired Agents Priceless

Motivated agents are priceless resources for call centers. In such a challenging and potentially monotonous job, agents need continuous inspiration, encouragement

Chapter 3

and recognition. Taking the 12 steps outlined here will help you to develop an incentive program that acknowledges call center agents' value and which motivates them to even higher levels of performance, contributes to overall organizational goals and enhances employee and customer satisfaction.

Rewards Programs Not Meeting Employee Needs

Incentive programs can be great motivators, but they won't reach their potential if there's a mismatch between an organization's overall rewards program and what agents are looking for.

According to a Towers Perrin survey, *Engaging Employees for Enhanced Performance: A New Role and Direction for Total Rewards*, many employees say that their organizations are not delivering the kinds of rewards they want and need.

A sample of 1,500 employees identified the importance of certain reward elements and how well their employer was delivering those elements. Their responses indicated a significant gap.

Call center managers might want to work with their HR departments to determine the rewards elements considered highly important by call center agents, and their perception of how well those elements are being delivered.

Company Program	Cited as Important by Employees	Being Met to Great Extent
Competitive Base Salary	84%	52%
Advancement Opportunities	72%	42%
Training Programs	72%	48%
Performance, Feedback, Coaching	71%	42%
Developmental Assignments	70%	47%
Variable Pay	69%	37%
Recognition Programs	53%	36%

Chapter 3

Chapter 4:
Career Pathing

Effective Career Progression Programs Balance Both Staff and Business Needs

by Susan Hash

The competition for skilled agents shows no signs of relenting. The increase in call center openings, available contact channels and types of agent skills required make it a job-seeker's market—and the outlook is pretty grim for call centers that don't have some type of agent development and retention process in place.

The historical corporate ladder approach to staff development has never been a viable option for call centers. After all, there are a finite amount of supervisory and management positions available.

Instead, a more effective staff-development approach is to prepare agents for the future of your business by taking into consideration individual staff needs and company goals. You'll also find that it's easier to get executive-level support and funding for call center career programs if they're aligned with overall business needs.

Depending on the type of advancement opportunities available in your organization and call center requirements, most centers follow one of two basic approaches to agent development. One focuses on an individualized acquisition of skill sets, while the other involves more structured tracks or levels through which agents can progress.

Identify the Skills Your Company Finds Desirable

AT&T's Consumer Services call centers (which include some 30 various-sized call centers nationwide) has created a career development program for its customer care reps called the Associate-to-Management Advancement Program (AMAP). It addresses two specific business needs that surfaced a few years ago:

• Local call centers recognized the need for a more disciplined approach to career progression (specifically, from the non-management account rep positions into management and supervisory positions), which would be perceived as objective by account reps.

Chapter 4

• AT&T wanted its management, organization-wide, to have consistent leadership skills. It developed a management-leadership framework, which consists of 10 competencies identified as the core leadership skills required for AT&T managers.

The call centers' AMAP process was designed with this framework in mind. "We wanted the people who were being promoted or hired into our call center management positions to have demonstrated the relevant competencies in this new management leadership framework," says Jerard Kehoe, sourcing and selection director for AT&T.

Differentiate Between Service and Management Skills

When developing a career-progression model, it's important to consider a path for agents who are not management- or career-oriented. "The reality is that there are some agents who are not interested in promotion, or who might not be viewed as potential candidates for promotion," says Jerard Kehoe, AT&T sourcing and selection director. "Success as a customer care rep does not necessarily predict success as a supervisor. The decision about how to develop reps into supervisors and which ones to select for promotion should be based on the skills that are relevant to supervision."

At Unum Provident Insurance, for instance, managers found that clear differentiators existed between being a senior-level rep and a specialist, says Anne O'Neil, call center director. For instance, some specific abilities identified were:
- Change management
- Problem identification and resolution
- Interaction with peers
- Conflict resolution
- Group leadership abilities.

To develop agents displaying management-type skills, the Unum Provident call centers created Mentor and Leadership Certification tracks in its career-progression model, with "distinct definitions of the behavior we're looking for and the competencies," O'Neil says. Agent progression in these areas is measured through 360-degree feedback and management observation.

Chapter 4

Skills-Based Development Relies on Individual Assessment

AT&T's AMAP essentially works as a skills-acquisition process in which agents can learn new skills at their own pace. At the same time, all of AMAP's phases are based on the management-leadership framework and target several of the skills outlined in it, such as planning and organizing, implementing with excellence and continuous learning.

In fact, as an individual moves up the AT&T management ladder, his or her performance continues to be appraised on that same framework, says Kehoe. "We've integrated AMAP with the other HR levers and strategies that represent the way AT&T wants to develop its managers—that's one of the program's strengths."

Candidates for the program are identified by the local supervisors who have the responsibility of coaching agents, not only for on-the-job performance, but also with an eye toward developing skills for eventual promotion.

The first stage of AMAP is called "Readiness Assessment." Supervisors assess agents' readiness to enter into the AMAP process based on their own judgment and the agent's past work behavior. The supervisor's evaluation also needs to be confirmed by the call center's local human resources manager.

After an agent is identified as being ready, he or she can participate in the next cycle of skills-assessment procedures, which are scheduled at each center two or three times a year.

Skill Paths Should Be Flexible to Meet Changing Caller Needs

Another company that has taken the skills-development approach to agent growth is Earthlink. The organization recently completed a merger with MindSpring Enterprises to create the second-largest Internet service provider in the United States with seven technical support call centers, which range from 150 to 500 agents.

Director of technical support Mark Hinkle describes Earthlink's skills-development process as similar to getting a college degree. Agents can take various classes; once they pass, they move on to the next course. While there is a slight hierarchy in the order of skills, the path is pretty varied depending on the agent's personal goals and customer needs.

Chapter 4

An important component of Earthlink's agent development program is the flexibility to react to changing customer demands, says Hinkle.

For instance, recently, the technical support organization expanded its agents' skills to focus on the Macintosh platform. "When the Apple iMac came out, the demand for Macintosh technical support just went through the ceiling," says Hinkle. "We've expanded the ability of our reps to take those calls. If we'd stayed with any kind of rigid hierarchy, we would be doing a disservice to our customers."

Group Skill Sets to Create a More Structured Career Path

A more structured approach to agent development calls for outlining specific levels or scales of progression and identifying the specific skill sets contained in each level.

While that seems like an overwhelming task "if you dig deep, you can find them," says Kim Weakley, assistant vice president and national call center manager at World Savings and Loan in San Antonio, Texas.

"But for the call centers that use skills-based routing, it becomes even easier. That's a very clear-cut way to build a career-progression model that will allow agents to grow," Weakley says.

In her call center, there are nine progression levels in the scale—three overall position levels and three sub-levels within each. For instance, Basic I, II and III Reps; Advanced I, II and III Reps; and Expert I, II and III Reps.

All new-hires are considered Basic I Reps. They're given an initial, eight-week training program in products, systems and customer service skills, as well as an overview of call center statistics "to understand the information we're going to be feeding back to them," she says.

After the first 90 days, new agents' skill levels are evaluated. At that point, most have reached the Basic III Rep level and they can sign up for the skills-assessment testing, which is conducted once a month.

Agents are individually coached by supervisors on the specific skills they need to progress to the next level. The call center also has an in-house team of trainers who work with agents on technical skills.

Unum Provident Insurance has developed a similar career path for staff at its centers. "We've created a trainee position for entry-level reps, plus a Rep I, Rep II and Specialists jobs," explains call center eirector Anne O'Neil.

Within each Rep job there are three tracks, each of which contains different skill sets based on various products. And the Specialist position contains three separate career paths agents can select:

1. Super reps are customer-focused agents who truly enjoy working in the call center on the phone dealing with customers. They generally want to acquire more product and systems knowledge, but aren't really interested in managing others. This path allows them to become subject-matter experts, cross-train on products and act as mentors for newer agents.

2. Training/quality/technology experts are trained to offer immediate internal support for the call center. "Even though we have support areas within I/T, it's beneficial to have people on staff with the ability to respond to technology issues quickly," says O'Neil. "They can often look at a situation with a system and get our people back on track within minutes vs. having to call something in and wait."

3. A leadership path is available for management-oriented agents. "We give them opportunities to participate in reviews, act as backup for management, attend meetings in place of managers and conduct call observations," she says.

Develop an Objective Assessment Process

One of the most critical aspects of an agent development program is an assessment process that's viewed as fair and unbiased by participants.

Kehoe feels that AT&T's AMAP assessment procedures make it distinct in that area. "It has formalized steps to objectively assess the skill levels the account reps have developed," he says. That process includes three events:

1. A written test that measures problem-solving and information-processing skills;

2. An "in-basket exercise" in which agents simulate being a manager by handling problem situations in a virtual in-basket; and

3. A discussion with a panel of trained interviewers who rate agents based on a pre-defined set of criteria.

Chapter 4

While testing procedures need to be consistently applied to avoid any appearance of favoritism, it's also important to know your agents, says World Savings' Weakley.

At her call center, agents go to a "test region" off the call center floor to process five to 10 customer requests, which can range from customer address changes to more complicated, sensitive issues like fixing checks that have been encoded incorrectly.

An unanticipated discovery with this process, however, was that some agents have "test phobia," she says. "They may be extremely proficient at performing certain types of tasks or calls on the floor, but when they know they're doing their monthly skills assessment, they freak out."

Weakley has worked around certain agents' test anxiety by using "sneak attacks." "We may give them something that needs to be done, and we don't tell them it's a skills assessment," she explains. The only potential hazard was that agents would be handling test issues live on the system, she points out, but adds that "we make sure we check it the same day, so we can delete those transactions and not impact the customer."

Extend Growth Possibilities Beyond the Call Center

If your agent development program is limited to your call center, at some point, you may find that you have a staff of highly trained experts—with no place else to go.

While the AT&T AMAP process is specifically focused on the progression from customer care rep to the entry-level call center supervisory position, agents who become qualified for entry-level management positions via the AMAP process can go into any number of positions that involve entry-level management within AT&T, says Kehoe. In fact, the organization has an internal post-and-bid staffing process that allows customer care reps to scan a staffing system for vacancies outside the call center in which they might be interested.

Earthlink's company culture also follows a promote-from-within philosophy, says Hinkle. In fact, he adds, "the majority of our company is staffed out of our call center. There are a lot of folks in executive-level positions who started out on the phones,

Chapter 4

including myself."

Typically, he says, agents move into areas like network operations, engineering, telecommunications and the MIS department.

Call center managers at Earthlink make a point of helping individual agents to progress and take into consideration any skills or interests agents have—even those not used in the call center. For instance, if an agent has an interest in Web design, their supervisor may give them a non-phone project to help showcase their skills for the company's Web Design Group.

Aligning Agent Programs Across Cultures and Centers

Mergers and acquisitions have a definite impact on agent-development programs in terms of growth potential, skills involved, job descriptions, promotional opportunities and the consistency of assessment. Trying to integrate two (or more) distinct points of view on staff development can be trying for managers when different cultures, customers and procedures are involved.

Last year, after Unum and Provident merged to create Unum Provident Insurance, managers were tasked with creating one agent-development program for the company's three call centers, located in Chattanooga, Tenn., Columbia, S.C.; and Portland, Maine, each of which served different types of customers.

At an initial planning meeting, which included representatives from each site, each manager detailed the programs currently in place at their centers. "We were trying to determine what would make sense [for all three centers]," she says. "It really came together based on what we heard from the agents in terms of their needs, and also what we, as the management team, felt we could manage. Each site had something that was a little different which we could leverage—and we took the best practices of each site."

The model was tested at the Portland call center to make sure it would work effectively and to give managers a chance to make adjustments. Next, O'Neil presented the model to an internal "roles group," which acts as a sounding board for programs developed around call center jobs, for more feedback and to identify any gaps in skills or job families. The final test was a review by the Human Resources department.

Eventually, O'Neil says, the goal is to bring other related areas under the same umbrella, such as a customer claims call center, employment call center, sales support center and a broker commissions group.

Chapter 4

Related company areas offer another avenue to boost agent growth. World Savings' call center extends agent learning through cross-training with its tax and insurance call center groups. It's a win-win for both areas, says Weakley. Her center trains reps from the tax and insurance groups to take calls when the volume gets heavy. At the same time, her agents cross-train on tax and insurance functions for those times when the tax group gets backed up. "Once we complete this, we're going to roll out a new skill level called a Universal Agent," she says.

Compensate Agents for Growth

Naturally, you can't expect agents to be motivated to learn and grow if there is no compensation for their efforts. Unless, of course, they're planning to take those skills elsewhere, which undermines your program's fundamental goal.

Agents at Unum Provident Insurance are assessed and certified for learning the skills included in their job-level tracks. After they've successfully demonstrated those skills on the job for six months, they receive a pay increase.

Because the program was just recently implemented, it's currently being self-funded with call center budget dollars. But, O'Neil says, since agent salaries were "not that far from where they needed to be, it's not a huge hit." However, she adds, based on the progression tracks that have been set up and the potential for retaining more experienced staff over the long term, her company's HR and finance managers have indicated that the future increases in compensation for agents are not unreasonable.

At World Savings, there are team and individual bonus opportunities associated with skills development. Pay-for-performance bonuses are paid quarterly to teams that reach pre-set expectations. Some goals are centerwide, such as service level objectives, while others focus on team projects and the skill level of team members. So, for instance, to get the team bonus, all members must be able to test at a certain skill level, such as Advanced I Rep.

Bonus opportunities for individual agents increase with each level, as well as for working less-desired shifts.

Here's how it works: An Advanced I Rep can receive a bonus of up to 2.1 percent of his or her salary; an Expert 3 can receive almost 5 percent. "There's quite a jump in compensation and it's incrementally staged going up the scale," says Weakley.

Also, in each of the categories, there is an A, B and C designation for shifts. For example, A is the 8 a.m. to 5 p.m. shift (highly desirable); B is 9 a.m. to 6 p.m.; and C is 10 a.m. to 7 p.m. (the least preferred shift). "We pay higher bonuses for C shifts," Weakley says.

"We try to cover all angles so that we can keep people on the less-preferred shifts, and there's an incentive to learn more on their own, be able to handle more tasks and create a greater repertoire of skills," she explains. "But we also want them to cover for each other—so if you have somebody who's a little bit slower at developing skills on your team, you're not going to bash them, you're going to help them. And it really has worked out well."

Do Agent Development Programs Impact Retention?

Absolutely, says Weakley. In 1998, her call center's turnover rate was between 55 to 60 percent. "We had a churning," she says. "We'd get them in and train them. They'd stay for six months and then they'd leave. We've dropped that rate to 17 percent."

AT&T is in the process of developing a plan to evaluate the effectiveness of the AMAP process, which has been in place for about two years. Kehoe points out that, based on employee satisfaction surveys, agents feel more positive about their progression opportunities. In addition, he says, "the early indications are that the people who are promoted via AMAP are demonstrating success in those management positions." Currently, about 670 Customer Care Reps have started the testing portion of the program. And of those, about 56 percent have successfully completed testing and have become qualified for promotion.

The effort of setting up a program is well worth it, says O'Neil. "Don't be afraid of negative thinking in the beginning or anything in your current environment that tells you it won't work," she says. "Just open up your thinking and be willing to explore all possibilities."

Chapter 4

Elements of a Successful Agent Development Program

by Anne Nickerson

"Career development... can be said to be at the core of human resource development. It requires the integration of human resource planning, assessment, selection and places appraisal, training, development, performance and reward management within the organizational structure and culture."

Marina Nordin
"Career Development and Planning Strategy," New Strait Times

Do you wonder if implementing a career path in your call center or company will make a difference in your staff morale and retention? Are you convinced that putting a career path in place is right, but don't know where to begin? Should you certify your agent, supervisory and management staff? Are you wondering whether or not the benefits will be worth the time, effort and expense? If you're grappling with any of these questions, read on for some thoughts and solutions you can take into consideration.

Will the Benefits Outweigh the Effort and Cost?

Many call center experts agree that the benefits do, in fact, far outweigh the efforts, resources and costs required to implement and maintain a career-path program. The result of a recent study by staffing services firm Manpower indicated that among the top motivators for call center personnel are the opportunities to learn new skills and to be offered continuous new challenges and support for personal growth.

And, as many managers can confirm, the more professionally you treat call center agents, the better they will treat their internal and external customers. Employees who are happy and satisfied with their jobs exude their confidence and satisfaction in the way that they approach and handle customers.

Chapter 4

Key Components of a Career Development Program

**Tips for Creating
a Successful Career Path**

Here are a few tips, suggestions and lessons learned from managers who have created effective career paths in their call centers.

- Create a project team consisting of human resource experts, agents and managers.
- Get buy-in to any changes you may make by inviting staff members representing each area of the call center to help design the program.
- Design, develop and implement quickly.
- Set and manage expectations.
- Create a formal and informal feedback process.
- Make adjustments quickly.
- Set up a mentoring program.
- Consider tuition reimbursement and local educational alliances.
- Determine policies regarding opportunities within and outside the department.
- Create a "marketing plan" to brand the image, and launch with "hoopla."
- Measure and publish results.

If you've already put individual agent performance plans and goals in place, implemented a quality assurance program and set up developmental coaching processes for your call center, then you've already made a strong start toward a career path program.

The next steps include identifying a progression of skills and measurements for increased complexity and job responsibility. Following are a few essential components for putting together your career path program.

First, identify the competencies, key skills, behaviors and attributes that are required for success on the job. One example may be "customer focus," which might include specific behaviors, such as the ability to:

- Identify caller needs;
- Acknowledge the impact of services and products (or lack of) on customer satisfaction;
- Use appropriate probing techniques;
- Find solutions;
- Follow through on customer requests using available resources; and
- Demonstrate a courteous attitude.

Once your competency model is identified, then "job clusters" need to be created. These are the specific job tasks in which the competencies are applied. They also become the foundation for your compensation planning.

Most career path options take a building-block approach where specific tasks need to be successfully accomplished in order to move from one level to the next. This often requires a well-thought-out pay and reward strategy where base pay increases drive skills acquisition, and some type of variable pay is linked to business results. In addition, a strong reward and recognition program should be created to continue to drive results—both individual and team—and maintain a culture that values learning. At a minimum, a successful program should outline expectations and standards, as well as the specific steps necessary to advance.

Some call centers align skills development with agent certification programs, which offer a clear outline for setting expectations and goals for staff, as well as a succession plan for the organization.

Certification programs also act as a form of reward and recognition for agents. Typically, agents receive diplomas or documentation (and sometimes monetary rewards) indicating that they have not only learned new skills and behaviors, but can apply them and maintain high performance on the job.

Training and Feedback Options

Besides outlining the development process, don't overlook two of the most critical components of any career-path program—the availability of training and performance feedback processes.

Many call centers have been very creative at offering high-quality options while keeping training costs to a minimum. For instance, some viable alternatives include partnering with local community institutions and educational programs, obtaining funds from economic development programs, using in-house experts or contracting for vendor-supplied programs.

While some centers have the resources to offer one-on-one coaching and mentoring, others take advantage of staff input, as well. An effective feedback method is 360-degree assessment, in which peers, teammates and supervisors offer individuals

Chapter 4

feedback for an objective, well-rounded view of a their performance.

Generally, most call center managers find that offering career development options gives agents a feeling of control over their destiny, increases their passion for their work and energizes them with a sense of pride about their achievements and optimism about their future. Call centers that have implemented career development programs find that they experience lower turnover, attract and retain high performers, and maintain high morale.

Focus on Skills Development, Rather than the Next Job

by Ellen Arrington

For a service culture to be sustained over the long term, people need more than slogans, ACD statistics and goals. They need room to grow professionally. The link between how agents are valued and developed and how they, in turn, treat customers is clear. When call centers invest the time to develop their staff, the positive benefits of that attention result in improved service for customers.

Many agents and team leaders want to broaden their skills in preparation for future growth, but they may be uncertain of how to go about doing so. As call center managers, we need to encourage this ambition and the energy that fuels it.

However, rather than focusing on the next job, we need to encourage agents to seek and develop their next set of skills. This requires us to do two things: 1) clarify the relationship between increased skills and the resulting career growth; and 2) provide leadership to help agents seek and develop new skills. By putting individual competence before discussions of the next promotion, we serve our staff—and organizations— more effectively. Agents will have the opportunity for advancement when their skills are improved, broadened and connected to the goals of the business.

Moving Beyond the Conventional Career Path

Managers often think in terms of a career path; instead, we need to focus on the *skill path* of both call center agents and team leaders. When we talk about pursuing a career, aren't we really talking about learning new competencies and building new skills in order to land the next position? Call centers provide many such opportunities. In fact, today's ideal call center career is not necessarily a ladder, but a path that moves laterally, as well as upward, with many interesting jobs along the way — enabling people to continually develop their competencies, build skills and grow in the organization.

People's desire for this type of skill-pathing enables the call center to attract good candidates and keep them in the fold. Agents and team leaders consistently rate

Chapter 4

learning and developing new skills among the top three attributes of a valued job.

How do call center supervisors and managers drive this skills acquisition? First, they define and communicate the competencies and skills required in each functional area of the call center. This shows agents what they need to learn before being viewed as candidates for lateral moves or advancement. Then supervisors and managers must clearly and constantly communicate the service levels, quality and production goals they want to achieve. Finally, and this is key, they must support and drive the development of each person's competencies and skills toward achieving those goals.

Take time during monthly call monitoring sessions to discuss the skills the agent is developing. Clarify the relationship between specific skills and the jobs or functions that require them. Set both skills-acquisition goals and the expectation that each agent will demonstrate new skill levels every quarter—or more often, if possible. Link skills development to performance reviews.

Show Agents the Call Center is Growth-Oriented

The result of such a skill-pathing approach is a passionate learning partnership that maximizes the performance of the call center and its people. The organization offers agents every chance to move forward with a growing company by providing learning opportunities and removing obstacles to cross-training for new functional areas. Agents reciprocate by taking charge of their own career and skills development—and, at the same time, deliver better service, reduce escalated calls through skilled handling of customers, uncover more sales referral opportunities and refer those opportunities at a higher rate. Best of all, as people gain experience and hone their abilities, they step into powerful roles in the organization rather than taking their services to the competition.

Tap the power of skill-pathing to send the message to your current agents and future prospects that your call center is a great place to learn and grow—and that you value their development. There is no better way to reward employees than with the new competencies and skills that set them up for success. And you'll be able to collect on your investment in their talents over the long term.

Empower Agents with the Resources and Authority to Satisfy Customers

by Susan Hash

What call center manager wouldn't want to have a staff of agents who proactively take personal responsibility for the customer's experience? Wishes aside, today it's a necessary element for business success.

Empowering frontline agents by providing them with the knowledge, skills and decision-making authority to take care of callers quickly and efficiently will enable them to represent your company as world class, says J.J. Lauderbaugh, president of Lauderbaugh & Associates Inc., a customer relations training and consulting firm in Los Gatos, Calif.

Empowered agents are more committed to the organization's success, she says. "They recognize that they're not just a part of customer service or support, but also involved in marketing and sales."

The nature of the multiple-channel call center environment demands an empowered workforce. The addition of a customer service Web site at HomeSide Lending Inc., a mortgage company headquartered in Jacksonville, Fla., demonstrated that necessity, according to HomeSide Lending's director of customer service Tom Reilly.

Although many of the simpler email responses to customers can be automated, there are more complex messages that include several inquiries. "Our email customer service agents have to be very skilled and empowered," Reilly says. "They have to have good discernment skills to ensure they're answering all of the customer's questions correctly in the first response."

Initial Obstacles to Overcome

Creating an empowered environment in which agents are focused on customer retention and call center productivity is a journey—and not without a few roadblocks at the start.

A focus group study of South Florida business leaders by Northwood University

Chapter 4

Empowerment Barriers

A study of employee empowerment in small businesses, conducted by Sam Houston State University, found five common barriers to empowerment:

• A lack of managerial commitment to the concept.

• An unwillingness to change on the part of the employee and/or manager.

• A reluctance on the part of employees to take on responsibility of making decisions.

• Poor communication between employees and managers.

• The failure to realize that, in the short run, performance may dip as empowerment is implemented.

revealed that nearly all of the participants said they encountered obstacles in launching empowerment processes. For instance, initially, both managers and staff resisted the effort. Many managers admitted they were reluctant to share decision-making activities with the front line, while others feared losing staff who develop new skills and capacities.

On the frontline side, the study found that staff who seldom had been given a voice in decision making often view the empowerment process with suspicion and distrust. The results further revealed that, at the beginning, organizations suffer a sharp drop in morale and productivity and an increase in turnover among managers and the front line.

Agent Buy-In Is Critical

"Frontline people who have never been given a high degree of responsibility are often afraid of it," says Lauderbaugh. "Or sometimes there's the view that empowerment just means having to do more work." Probably one of the biggest fears for newly empowered frontline agents is that they will be reprimanded (or worse) for making mistakes.

To get agents to accept decision-making power, Lauderbaugh says it's important to clearly communicate the specific advantages to the agents of learning new skills and taking on more responsibility. The ability to advance in their careers is a particularly attractive benefit. At electric appliance manufacturer Braun Inc., the empowerment process offers consumer service reps a visible career growth opportunity. Reps can advance through three tiers to become product specialists, says consumer service manager Ann-Marie O'Keefe. In fact, two of the department's current supervisors were promoted from within, which "is very encouraging for new reps," she says.

Of course, not all agents are the same when it comes to decision-making abilities. "You must know them well enough to understand who is trained and capable of taking responsibility," Lauderbaugh says. Often that has to do with whether or not an individual is goal-oriented. She suggests screening for goal-oriented agents during the recruiting process by asking each candidate what he or she has won in the past. "If someone can't come up with anything that he or she has ever won, they're probably not goal-oriented," she explains. "They haven't given up something to win something."

Different Types of Empowerment

To build an empowered culture, agents need clear decision-making guidelines for dealing with customers. For instance, what's the dollar limit for returns? Can they give away free products? What options can they offer to customers?

Braun consumer service reps have specific policies and procedures for handling different types of product calls. "Our reps are empowered to make decisions, such as whether or not to extend a warranty, provide a repair or a replacement," says O'Keefe. "We don't want callers to have to go to a supervisor for that—it's within the reps' realm of responsibility."

Besides service support, Braun's empowerment process involves product knowledge. The company's 22 consumer service reps are encouraged to learn as much as they can about the various products. (Braun has eight product lines, which include hundreds of appliances and products.) Agents can borrow products to take home and get familiar with them, or they can buy them at a discount.

Through the career progression process, reps can train to become product specialists, becoming responsible for training the rest of the department on their specific products and handling any out-of-the-ordinary calls involving those products.

Agents at HomeSide Lending's Jacksonville call center also increase their level of responsibility as they advance within the center, says Jeanne Babbitt, Jacksonville call

Chapter 4

center manager. Senior and lead agents are empowered to make more risky decisions than the typical frontline agents. "They provide a support function to the supervisor as well as the phone reps," Babbitt says.

Another position in the center is that of mentor, which is "a very empowered rep who can make supervisory-type decisions and support reps with more complex issues," Bobbitt explains.

Training and Feedback Are Key

A study conducted by Sam Houston State University found training to be an inherent element of empowerment. A well-defined training process ensures "the development of employee skills, as well as the exchange of information about job requirements, organizational performance and customer satisfaction," the study reports.

"Our training and empowerment process starts the minute the rep walks in the door," says HomeSide Lending's Babbitt. Call center supervisors sit in on new-hire training (which is conducted by corporate training staff) to ensure that it's on target for the call center. "They audit the training content (as well as the response from the class) to make sure it's going to meet our needs once those reps hit the floor in the call center," she explains. Managers meet with the training staff on a monthly basis to give them feedback on new-hires' progress. "We also provide our training staff with a list of primary call drivers to incorporate into the training to help reps meet customers' needs," Bobbitt says.

The company's ongoing training process, about 35 hours a year, includes team training, event-driven training (i.e., government regulatory changes, year-end mortgage process changes, etc.) and updates on soft skills.

Continuously Identify Empowerment Opportunities

HomeSide's empowerment process includes a 360-degree review of rep training. Customer service mentors, who support frontline reps, log any calls they receive from reps. The logs are checked regularly to find out how many calls mentors received, from whom and why. Managers can then identify which reps may need

Chapter 4

additional training, says Tom Reilly. In addition, mentor calls are further dissected to determine any overall training gaps.

The reps themselves can identify empowerment opportunities in focus group sessions that meet on a regular basis or are pulled together for a specific function. "We have focus groups targeted to customer service functions that we handle, such as taxes or insurance. The reps have a very vocal voice in identifying what the empowerment issues are," says Reilly.

In another program, called "Voice of the Customer," reps are encouraged to electronically share caller comments—good or bad—that may be improvement opportunities or simply customer kudos.

How Empowered Do Your Agents Feel?

Before beginning an empowerment process, it's important first to assess your call center's needs, as well as your agents' feeling of empowerment with their jobs, says Allen Klose, author of *Breaking the Chains: The Empowerment of Employees— How to Evaluate, Monitor and Improve Employee Empowerment Levels.* Klose suggests conducting a survey that looks at the following areas:

- How empowered do our agents feel?
- Do empowerment levels differ greatly within the department?
- Do our supervisors have different levels of empowerment than our frontline agents?
- Can we develop the specific programs necessary to improve empowerment among our agents?
- If empowerment levels are high, how will this change our strategy of increasing agent involvement?

Encourage Agent Involvement

Getting agents engaged with other departments helps to foster a sense of commitment to the company. Braun's product specialists act as a liaison between consumer services and marketing. They attend marketing meetings, as well as regularly communicate with the marketing department via email or phone, says O'Keefe.

Product specialists regularly review call data to pinpoint common product issues and offer suggestions to the marketing, quality or technical services departments.

Reps also are encouraged to offer their suggestions for improving processes, such

Chapter 4

as order turnaround, shipping issues, etc. "The reps are better able to recognize issues quickly because they're the front line," says O'Keefe. "We encourage them not to wait until it shows up on our reports but to constantly share their feedback. Over time, agents become very knowledgeable at all levels. Knowledge is power, and it gives them the ability to handle any issue that comes their way."

Managers Have Responsibilities, Too

Empowerment is not simply a matter of delegating tasks. For call center managers, the leadership responsibilities evolve.

"Managers need to be role models to the agents in the call center," says Lauderbaugh. "They need to focus on growing, mentoring, coaching and counseling their people. As agents witness the empathy supervisors feel for them, as well as concern for their individual growth, they will have a tendency to treat the customers the same way. All call center managers should treat their agents the same as they want their agents to treat callers," she says.

"You have to listen to your employees and your customers," adds Jeanne Babbitt. "Sometimes managers are afraid to give up control but, in the long run, it increases employee satisfaction and customer satisfaction."

Reilly agrees. "That customer satisfaction translates into bottom-line savings. One-stop calls are definitely the way to go, and if you empower reps so that they can answer the call and provide a solution that does not result in more calls, then we are dollars and dollars ahead of where we need to be.

"With rep empowerment, you never quite get to the destination because you're always finding new opportunities because of the changing nature of the business that we're in. I encourage my staff not to be satisfied—there's always something more that you can do."

Changing Agent Development Opportunities in the Multichannel Environment

by Wanda Sitzer

As customer touch-points evolve from the simplicity of voice-only contact to the more complex email, text-chat and online videophone interactions, the call center industry must embrace more sophisticated profiling, training and management techniques.

Mundane tasks can be handled by self-service functions, leaving your agents free to develop relationships that require more involvement and skill than merely issuing templated responses.

We have to acknowledge our contact-interaction representatives for the awesome responsibility they fulfill in shaping customers' experiences and delivering on companies' brand promises and service commitments in a multimedia environment.

The Elements of E-Skill Training

Employing representatives proficient in "CyberSpeak" or "NetSpeak"—a language far different from the formal prose taught in high school language classes, and yet, not as informal as phone conversations encouraged in our interaction centers—will differentiate the companies that thrive vs. those that only survive.

An e-skill set can be cultivated with your existing staff through practice and aptitude. However, practice does require time away from the phones (not just on-the-job training), which is a stretch for call centers, but not a luxury.

Reps need to practice electronic communication tasks, such as categorizing email and determining whether messages require templated responses and which ones require customization. Honing perceptivity to decipher customer needs and customer tone in a brief written message is no simple task. Add the element of speed for text-chat sessions and online navigating, plus focus and concentration for handling multiple sessions—and everyone will agree that multichannel interaction centers require a sophisticated combination of skills.

Chapter 4

Align Service Interactions with Company Image

In addition to proper grammar usage, reps need to be able to embrace language that jives with the soul of the organization. In too many companies, customer service has been homogenized to the point of "smile skills"—saying the company name at the beginning and end of the call, and using the customer's name at least once in the conversation.

Web interaction, phone interaction, packaging, direct marketing and awareness ads should all line up. If we live by the premise that says that customers want to do business with us, in part, because of how we've presented ourselves through marketing then, indeed, they won't be turned off when we let a little of our essence into the quality exchange—rather they'll bask in it. It will confirm to our callers that we are who they thought we were, and that the company experience is what they imagined it would be.

Companies should consider more special ways of handling online and phone interactions rather than seeking a routine, consistent, generic manner. For instance, the title for help desk agents at www.techknow-how.com is "techknowledgist," which says it all. Or how about "egreetologist"? That's what reps at Egreetings are called. Titles like these make sense and change the tenor of the conversation—which reps can live up to with unique company brand training.

> ### A Return to Visual Service
>
> At the visual end of the multiple-channel spectrum, a challenge for call centers will be turning the multimillion-dollar brand messages and packaging into consistent experiences when delivered "in virtual person."
>
> Some outsourcing companies are using video technology to convey a sense of confidence to customers in complicated interactions like technical support.
>
> Soon, training call center reps will need to incorporate customer service lessons on face-to-face service and visual feedback topics, such as: "How to Show You're Listening and How to Look Interested."
>
> E-plays and virtual-plays (medium-specific role-plays) should be common nomenclature for recruiters as they seek professional representatives who can communicate and perform comfortably across various media.

Chapter 4

Multiple Channels and Skills Builds a Case for Higher Pay

Awarding commensurate salaries is essential if our reps are to succeed in elevating the call center image and cementing the brand relationship. Call centers can build a case at the CEO level that reps breathe life into the customer experience and bring a return on investment to executives' brand promises. This complex professional competency requires respect and an environment in which reps can feel the effects of their contributions—a leading job motivator.

The challenges for call centers are to design career paths, interaction institutions and creative settings that will attract high-quality candidates in a tight labor market and nurture and retain our most valuable asset.

Impact of Call Center Size and Industry Type on Agent Growth and Career Opportunities

by Maggie Klenke

If there is one thing we can depend on in the call center world, it is change. Inbound call centers that used to handle phone calls, fax and correspondence are evolving into multimedia centers with email, Web and video transactions. Simply servicing the customers' requests is no longer enough—now we're also focusing on maximizing the entire customer relationship, increasing wallet share and customer retention.

And frontline agents are taking on the responsibility of complex transactions, while automated systems take care of the easy ones. Add to that record-low unemployment, which makes it harder and harder to attract and retain the kind of personnel needed.

Clearly, the agents who have been with the center for a while are seeing the changes, too. They're required to learn new skills to ensure their place in the new customer interaction center (CIC). Training plans and career paths need to be established to maximize and retain these agents.

True, some agents recruited originally for phone work may never make the transition to handling Web and/or video transactions. Likewise, some of your best email service reps ought not to be asked to handle a phone call. But the opportunities to grow and develop need to be made available to as many as possible.

The Role of Call Center Size and Volume on Skill Groups

The size of the center staff will have a direct bearing on the center's ability to offer effective growth plans. A large center can tolerate more people who have very specific skills, while a smaller group needs more agents with the capability to handle as many transaction types as possible.

It's a simple case of economies of scale. If you have 100 agents, you can afford to have some who only handle phone calls, while others deal specifically with email. And skills-based routing will allow you to utilize a broad range of skill combinations effectively. But if you have only 15 agents, specialists can be a real problem in scheduling and ensuring coverage for the peaks and valleys of demand for each contact medium.

Likewise, another consideration is the number of products or services your center supports. For instance, if there are three or four types of products or services and four to five different media choices, everyone needs to be able to handle several of each to ensure decent response times and a good match of agent skill to customer needs. While a skills-based routing plan may still be an effective tool to use, the choices need to be simpler.

Also, there may be more opportunities for agents to maximize their training and vary their workloads in small call centers, while larger centers concentrate more on depth, rather than breadth, of skill.

Call center size can also influence how motivated different types of agents will be. For instance, agents who thrive on challenge, change and variety are ideal for universal agent positions. Agents with more limited capabilities and/or less ambition may still be major contributors in large centers that can keep them busy in their specialty. And a "super rep" needs an environment where becoming an expert in a narrow field can be encouraged and effectively utilized (which is the larger center).

Industry Type Can Indicate Skill Vs. Career Paths

What impact does type of industry have on agent-development programs? In an industry where the customer contacts are very simple and repetitive (say, a messaging center for a paging company), the challenges to learn new things are few and growth opportunities limited. In this case, moving up into a supervisory position has more potential than expecting challenging content in the contacts or multimedia transactions. Here, the career progression is clearly a management path or movement out of the center for growth-oriented agents.

However, in a highly complex environment, like a technical support help desk, the challenges come so fast and furious it is almost impossible to keep up with all of them. New operating systems, new applications, complex interactions with customers via the Web, email and phone are the norm. In this type of environment, a technically inclined agent can find plenty of challenges and career growth without having to consider personnel management, if that is not their forte.

It is fair to say that most centers will find themselves somewhere in the middle of the relatively extreme examples above. They will need to develop meaningful career paths and skill development plans for their agents, and customize them to the individuals as well.

Planning a development path for those who have no interest in people management will allow you to retain experienced technical folks who are the backbone of the center. And identifying growth plans for those who do want to go into management may have to include movement to other jobs in the company if there are not enough promotional opportunities in the center. After all, it's better to have them move up in the company than lose them to the competition.

Overall, the size of your call center and your industry type certainly will play important roles in establishing an effective career and skill development process. But the most important thing is to develop a plan that takes different growth paths into consideration and to make sure everyone in your center knows what that is and how to achieve the results desired.

Chapter 4

Chapter 5:
Humor

A Brief Guide to Progressive Agent Incentives and Recognition

Spicing Up the Agent Image

A Brief Guide to Progressive Agent Incentives and Recognition

By Greg Levin

Numerous studies have shown that agents who feel overstressed, underpaid and unappreciated treat customers poorly, make numerous errors and are three times more likely than happy agents to set a supervisor on fire. In fact, of the 15 incidents where call center supervisors caught fire last year, 14 were caused by agents with low morale (the 15th incident was the result of a vacationing supervisor who got careless during a volcano expedition).

Call centers without innovative incentives and recognition practices often incur astronomical turnover rates and poor customer loyalty. Yet few centers have implemented truly progressive practices that inspire agents to achieve organizational objectives and to forget the fact that they are chained to cubicles.

Here are a few examples of what I believe are the most creative and promising motivational tactics around. (Note: Some of these ideas are still a bit unrefined. You may want to first test them out on lab mice or a select group of agents you particularly dislike).

Executive Suites for Top Performers

You can't expect agents to feel proud and continually meet the high demands placed on them if they continue to be shackled to cramped workstations in a warehouse environment. You need to show them that they are just as valuable to the company as the CEO. That's why I suggest building an octagonal-shaped call center where your top eight performers each get to work in a corner office.

Agents will knock themselves out on the phones to earn the right to occupy one of these "executive suites." To sweeten the pot and to provide agents with a real feeling of power, you can also give those who attain "agent executive" status a key to the executive washroom, permit them to speak to customers via speakerphone and give them the right to completely ignore the rest of the call center staff.

It's best to rotate top performers in and out of the executive suites on a weekly or monthly basis. Longer stays may cause agents to get cocky and start recommending staffing cuts negotiating mergers.

Radical Title Change

Another great way to make agents feel important and valued is to change their job titles to something that commands more respect.

Instead of the bland "agent" or "rep," try something creative like "Headset Honcho," "Contact King," "Queue Queen" or the increasingly popular, "The Artist Formerly Known as Operator."

You'd be amazed at how a radical title change can impact motivation and performance. For example, a catalog call center in Eau de Formage, Wis., recently conducted a revealing experiment where it separated agents into three groups, giving the agents in each group a different title: 1) "Agent"; 2) "Customer Specialist"; and 3) "Service Overlord."

The results were remarkable: The "Agent" group achieved mediocre service levels, reported high turnover and set two supervisors on fire. The "Customer Specialist Group" faired better—achieving average service levels with a moderate rate of turnover and only set one supervisor on fire. In comparison, the "Service Overlord" group exceeded all service level objectives, had zero turnover and quickly extinguished the three supervisor fires.

Spell-Based Pay Program

Two unfortunate call center facts:

- Most agent salaries wouldn't even pay for one of the CEO's golf clubs; and
- Most agents can't even spell "CEO" when writing customer email.

One of the best ways to enhance agent wages (and retention rates) while, at the same time, improving your center's email response quality is to introduce a formal "spell-based pay" program.

Here's how it works: For every correctly spelled word in an agent's email response, you pay them 5 cents—or 1 cent if you manage a service bureau. Not only will such a program enable agents to earn some much-needed additional money and inspire them to improve, it will greatly reduce the chances of your call center being paid an angry visit by editors from Merriam-Webster.

The only real drawback of a spell-based pay program is that as agents' writing improves, they may earn enough money to buy a newspaper and find other job opportunities in the area.

Spicing Up the Agent Image

By Greg Levin

Many call center professionals have told me that they are struggling more than ever to attract qualified agent applicants. My typical piece of advice, "Wear something sexy" – which, by the way, used to get big laughs – now causes managers to merely growl and tell me to grow up. They're fed up with having to recruit from a shallow labor pool, and even my sophisticated wit isn't enough to get them to crack a smile anymore.

The big problem is the negative image that most young people have of call center work: sitting in small, gray cubicles while wearing an uncomfortable headset and answering call after call after call for hours on end, with little room for advancement. But that's such a distorted view. For instance, some cubicles today are a nice shade of blue.

Okay, let's face it, as rewarding as call center work may be, on the surface it's not that alluring to college graduates or others with strong communication skills and serious debt. Here are some suggestions to help spice-up the industry image and enhance the chances of you having to tell alumni from schools like Stanford and Brown that you'll keep their resume on file in case an agent position opens up.

1. Provide "alternative" headsets. Many young people feel that wearing a headset is a sign of failure, an indication that they are just a lowly "operator" lacking any real skills. They fail to realize that 1) being a call center agent requires numerous important skills; 2) even CEOs wear headsets during long calls to avoid stiff necks; and 3) four out of five medical doctors surveyed say that wearing a headset significantly decreases the chances of having a bee fly into your ear while on the job.

But rather than try to overcome the general public's negative view of headsets, why not replace the devices with something that doesn't really look like a headset. For example, you could decorate each headset with fake diamonds, rubies and emeralds. Then, whenever you meet reluctant applicants who feel they are "above" call center work, you can tell them they'll get to wear a bejeweled crown to fit their royal self-image.

2. Break up the monotony. Most people are turned off by call center work because the thought of handling calls from the average Joe all day long makes them yawn. They want something more exciting and unpredictable. I say give them what they want. Do creative things like occasionally hire an actor to play a disgruntled customer who runs into the call center screaming obscenities and threatening the lives of any agent who moves from their seat. This will not only get staff's adrenaline pumping and make them tell their friends (potential applicants) how invigorating their job is, it will reduce the amount of "wandering" agents engage in, thus improving adherence-to-schedule statistics.

Other easy ways to inject excitement into the agents' call center routine include 1) sponsoring unannounced "nude supervisor" days; 2) releasing a rabid wolverine on the phone floor; and 3) moving the call center to Rio during the Carnival.

3. Create a sitcom about agents in a call center. One of the best ways to attract young people to call center work is to make it the subject of a hit comedy TV sitcom, preferably starring Michael Richards from *Seinfeld* as the zany lead agent. I urge call center professionals throughout the industry to get together and create such a show, and call it something like *Mad About Queue* or *Ain't Life a Kick in the Headset*. All that's needed is about 10 good-looking mediocre actors wearing cool clothes, a New York City or Los Angeles setting, some call center props and, of course, a rabid wolverine or two.

Each episode could highlight typical call center occurrences, with a little embellishment to enhance ratings. For instance, the pilot episode could be about how the agents—struggling to handle the call volume—kidnap the CEO's wife and golf clubs until he agrees to staffing increases.

I recommend contacting the head of the Fox Television Network to get this baby on TV. There should be no problem winning his approval, provided that you follow the Fox formula and promise that all characters will sleep with one another before the end of the first season.

Note: If all else fails in your attempts to attract hordes of agent applicants, consider paying off the Surgeon General to declare that NOT handling dozens of calls a day from customers can cause baldness and bad breath.

Index

Publication Dates

How to Reach the Publisher

We would love to hear from you! How could this book be improved? Has it been helpful? No comments are off limits! You can reach us at:

Mailing Address: Call Center Press, a division of ICMI, Inc.
P.O. Box 6177
Annapolis, MD 21401

Telephone: 410-267-0700, 800-672-6177

Fax: 410-267-0962

Email: icmi@incoming.com

Web site: www.incoming.com

About ICMI, Inc.

Incoming Calls Management Institute (ICMI), based in Annapolis, Maryland, offers the most comprehensive educational resources available for call center (contact center, interaction center, help desk) management professionals. ICMI's focus is helping individuals and organizations understand the dynamics of today's customer contact environment in order to improve performance and achieve superior business results. From the world's first seminar on incoming call center management, to the first conference on call center/Internet integration and subsequent research on multichannel integration, ICMI is a recognized global leader. Quality, usability and value have become trademarks of ICMI's award-winning services. ICMI is independent and is not associated with, owned or subsidized by any industry supplier; ICMI's only source of funding is from those who use its services.

ICMI's services include:

- Public and onsite (private) seminars
- Web seminars and e-learning courses
- Certification review seminars and study guides
- Industry studies and research papers
- Consulting services
- Software tools for scheduling and analysis
- Books (including the industry's best-selling book, *Call Center Management on Fast Forward*)
- QueueTips, the popular (and free) monthly e-newsletter
- Membership in Incoming Calls Management Institute
- *Call Center Management Review*, the authoritative monthly journal for ICMI members

For more information and to join a network of call center leaders, see www.incoming.com

Incoming Calls Management Institute
Post Office Box 6177
Annapolis, Maryland 21401
410-267-0700 • 800-672-6177
icmi@incoming.com
www.incoming.com

Author Biographies

Ellen Arrington is vice president of Omega Performance Corp., a call center consulting firm based in Sausalito, Calif. Ellen has more than 24 years of training and organizational development expertise, and has managed the design and implementation of all training programs for the startup of Charles Schwab's call centers.

Dan Coen is call center manager for Blue Shield of California's call center in Los Angeles. He is a published author as well as a management workshop leader. Dan specializes in cultivating agent teams and developing proven incentive/compensation plans to enhance quality and productivity.

Christian Ellis is a senior consultant in Sibson & Company's Cary, North Carolina office and helps call centers enhance performance via their human capital.

Leslie Hansen Harps is a freelance business writer specializing in customer service and call centers. She is the former president of the Customer Service Institute, and author of several books.

Susan Hash is the editor-in-chief of *Call Center Management Review*. She has been a business journalist/writer for 15 years, and has received several journalism awards for reporting on the customer service industry.

Elizabeth Hawk is a principal and one of the leaders of the organizational performance and rewards practice at Sibson & Co., a firm specializing in call center effectiveness and compensation consulting.

Maggie Klenke is managing director of the Customer Interaction Center consulting practice of Getronics. She teaches seminars on a variety of call center and telecommunications topics and is a frequent speaker at industry events and trade shows.

Greg Levin is the former editor of *Call Center Management Review*. Greg is a regular contributor to the publication, and also writes the "In Your Ear" call center humor column. He is currently a freelance writer based in Spain.

Julia Mayben is a freelance writer based in Annapolis, Md. She is a regular contributor to *Call Center Management Review*, and is co-author of *Call Center Management on Fast Forward*.

Anne Nickerson is president of Call Center Coach, which provides call center professionals with comprehensive resources for human resource development processes.

Wanda Sitzer is executive vice president and co-founder of Initiatives Three Inc., a consulting firm specializing in phone and Web initiatives to improve customer service, marketing and sales management.

Fay Wilkinson is a senior partner with Questeq Learning Programs, an Orangeville, Ontario-based consulting firm specializing in helping call centers achieve their training and performance objectives. Fay has 30 years' experience in customer service and call centers, and has spoken at numerous industry conferences and seminars.

Order Form

QTY.	Item	Price	Total
	ICMI Handbook and Study Guide Series Module 1: People Management*** Module 2: Operations Management*** Module 3: Customer Relationship Management*** Module 4: Leadership and Business Management***	 $199.00 $199.00 $199.00 $199.00	
	Call Center Management On Fast Forward: Succeeding In Today's Dynamic Inbound Environment Book** Cassette set, 6 tapes** Book and Cassette tape set bundle***	 $34.95 $49.95 $69.95	
	Call Center Technology Demystified: The No-Nonsense Guide to Bridging Customer Contact Technology, Operations and Strategy**	 $39.95	
	Topical Books: **The Best of** *Call Center Management Review* Call Center Recruiting and New Hire Training* Call Center Forecasting and Scheduling* Call Center Agent Motivation and Compensation* Call Center Agent Retention and Turnover*	 $16.95 $16.95 $16.95 $16.95	
	Industry Studies Monitoring Study Final Report II (published 2002)* Multichannel Call Center Study (published 2001)* Agent Staffing and Retention Study (published 2000)*	 $99.00 $99.00 $79.00	
	Forms Books Call Center Sample Monitoring Forms* Call Center Sample Customer Satisfaction Forms Book*	 $49.95 $49.95	
	Software QueueView: A Staffing Calculator – CD ROM* Easy Start™ Call Center Scheduler Software – CD-ROM*	 $49.00 $299.00	
	Call Center Manager's Jump-Start Toolkit****	$279.00	
	Call Center Humor: The Best of *Call Center Management Review* Volume 3*	$9.95	
	The Call Centertainment Book*	$8.95	
	Shipping & Handling @ $5.00 per US shipment, plus .50¢ per* item, $1.00 per** item, $2.00 per*** item and $3.00 per**** item. Additional charges apply to shipments outside the US.		
	Tax (5% MD residents, 7% GST Canadian residents)		
	TOTAL (US dollars)		

Please contact us for quantity discounts

For more information on our products, please visit **www.incoming.com**

❑ Please send me a free issue of *Call Center Management Review* (ICMI's journal for members) and information on ICMI's publications, services and membership.

Please ship my order and/or information to:

Name _____

Title _____

Industry _____

Company _____

Address _____

City_____State _____Postal Code _____

Telephone ( ) _____

Fax ( ) _____

Email_____

Method of Payment (if applicable)

❑ Check enclosed (Make payable to ICMI Inc.; U.S. Dollars only)

❑ Charge to: ❑ American Express ❑ MasterCard ❑ Visa

Account No. _____

Expiration Date _____

Name on Card _____

Fax order to: 410-267-0962
call us at: 800-672-6177
410-267-0700
order online at: www.incoming.com
or mail order to: ICMI Inc.
P.O. Box 6177, Annapolis, MD 21401

ICMI's Membership Program

Join your peers, industry veterans and management professionals in the call center industry's most helpful membership program!

Incoming Calls Management Institute's Membership Program helps its members enhance their management abilities by offering the best resources, networking opportunities and management tools. Whether your job focuses on people management, workforce management, technology or strategy, the ICMI Membership Community is dedicated to meeting your needs.

Benefits of ICMI Membership include:

- Exclusive access to our online Membership site
- Free access to our online "KnowledgeBase" of over 500 articles
- Education-oriented conferences dedicated to developing your call center knowledge
- Monthly subscription to *Call Center Management Review*
- Discounts on all ICMI seminars, publications, events and conferences
- The online ICMI Membership Directory
- The ability to network with industry leaders, stay abreast of industry developments and develop your management abilities

Plus, you can custom-tailor your membership by choosing the Professional Interest Area (s) most relevant to your needs. These include:

- Workforce Management
- People Management
- Technology Management
- Strategy and Leadership

How do I sign up?

To become a member of ICMI's Membership Program, or to learn more about the program's details, please visit the members' website at www.icmimembers.com, or call us toll free at 800-672-6177 or 410-267-0700.

QueueTips™

Building Community and Conversation
Between Call Center Leaders Worldwide

ICMI's free interactive email bulletin provides a forum for call center leaders to share questions and answers, experiences and tips. This online question and answer "knowledgebase" provides a host of proven and tested solutions for call center management issues and offers insight into how professionals like you have addressed problems and pursued opportunities to achieve success.

Hundreds of questions and responses have been posted. A small sampling of the topics include:

• How Can I Combat Staff Turnover?
• Why Do My Abandonment Rates Differ?
• How Can We Improve the Accuracy of our Forecast?
• How Do I Create A Career Path?

But remember, QueueTips is more than just a databank of answers. Registered participants are encouraged to submit questions or scenarios that require assistance, advice or just a fresh perspective. Think of it as a collective conscience of the Call Center Industry!

Signing up for QueueTips is free and easily accomplished. Just go to our website at www.incoming.com, or call us toll free at 800-672-6177 or 410-267-0700 to sign up!